Andrew Burnaby, Francis Fauquier

Travels Through the Middle Settlements in North-America,

in the Years 1759 and 1760

With observations upon the state of the colonies

Andrew Burnaby, Francis Fauquier

Travels Through the Middle Settlements in North-America, in the Years 1759 and 1760
With observations upon the state of the colonies

ISBN/EAN: 9783337292317

Printed in Europe, USA, Canada, Australia, Japan

Cover: Foto ©Andreas Hilbeck / pixelio.de

More available books at **www.hansebooks.com**

TRAVELS

THROUGH THE

MIDDLE SETTLEMENTS

IN

NORTH AMERICA,

IN THE YEARS 1759 AND 1760.

WITH

OBSERVATIONS

UPON THE

STATE OF THE COLONIES.

BY THE REV. ANDREW BURNABY, A.M.
VICAR OF GREENWICH.

LONDON:
Printed for T. PAYNE, at the Mews Gate.
MDCCLXXV.

INTRODUCTION.

A Few days before I embarked for America, being in a coffee-house with some friends, and discoursing of things relative to that country, an elderly gentleman advancing towards the box where we were sitting, addressed himself to me in the following manner: "Sir," said he, "you are young, "and just entering into the world; I am old, and upon the "point of leaving it: allow me therefore to give you one piece "of advice, which is the result of experience, and which may "possibly, some time or other, be of use to you. You are "going to a country where every thing will appear new and "wonderful to you; but it will appear so only for a while; "for the novelty of it will daily wear off; and in time it will "grow quite familiar to you. Let me, therefore, recommend "to you to note in your pocket-book every circumstance, that "may make an impression upon you; for be assured, sir, though "it may afterward appear familiar and uninteresting to your- "self, that it will not appear so to your friends who have never "visited that country, and that they will be entertained by it."

The following observations were the result of this advice: they were written upon the several spots to which they refer; and were intended for no other purpose, than that of serving as memorandums. They appeared, by the time that I returned to Europe, according to the gentleman's prediction, so very familiar to me, that I scarcely thought them deserving of the

INTRODUCTION.

perufal of my friends. Some of thefe, however, were fo obliging as to beftow upon them that trouble; and it is by their advice, and the confideration of the prefent critical fituation of affairs, that I now fubmit them to the judgment of the public.—Whatever may be their merit, which I fear is but fmall, one thing I can affure the reader of, I believe, they are generally true. They are the fruit of the moft impartial inquiries, and beft intelligence, that I was able to procure in the different colonies which I vifited. If I have been led into any error, or mifreprefented any thing, it has been undefignedly: a fpirit of party is univerfally prevalent in America, and it is not always an eafy matter to arrive at the knowledge of truth; but I believe, in general, I have been pretty fuccefsful. I converfed indifcriminately with perfons of all parties, and endeavoured, by allowing for prejudices and collating their different accounts, to get at the true one. If I have any doubt myfelf about any particular part of the following obfervations (and it is one in which I wifh I may be found to have been mifinformed), it is that which relates to the character of the Rhode-Iflanders. I was exceedingly ill at that place, and had not the fame opportunity of procuring information as elfewhere. I converfed with but few gentlemen in that colony, and they were principally of one party, but they were gentlemen of fuch univerfal good character, that I could not but rely in fome meafure on the accounts which they favoured me with. Some allowance, however, I did make for prejudice, and I am defirous that the reader fhould make a ftill larger one; indeed, I fhould be

happy

INTRODUCTION.

happy to ftand corrected in regard to what I have faid of that people, as no one can have lefs pleafure in fpeaking unfavourably of mankind than myfelf.

I have ftudioufly avoided all technical or fcientific terms; fuch to the informed reader are unneceffary, to the uninformed one they are ufelefs and perplexing: in relations of this kind, they have always an appearance of affectation and pedantry.

For the moft valuable part of the following collection, I mean the Diary of the Weather, I am intirely indebted to my efteemed friend, Francis Fauquier efq, fon to the late worthy lieutenant-governor of Virginia, who very obligingly tranfmitted it to me from Williamfburg, while I was chaplain to the Britifh factory at Leghorn; and has allowed me to make the ufe of it which I have here done.

The prefent unhappy differences fubfifting amongft us, with regard to America, will, I am fenfible, expofe the publication of this account to much cenfure and criticifm; but I can truly aver, that I have been led to it, by no party motive whatfoever. My firft attachment, as it is natural, is to my native country; my next is to America; and fuch is my affection for both, that I hope nothing will ever happen to diffolve that union, which is fo neceffary to their common happinefs. Let every Englifhman and American, but for a moment or two, fubftitude themfelves in each other's place, and, I think, a mode of reconciliation will foon take effect.—Every American will then perceive the reafonablenefs, of acknowledging the fu-

premacy

premacy of the British legislature; and every Englishman perhaps, the hardship of being taxed where there is no representation, or assent.

There is scarcely any such thing, I believe, as a perfect government, and solecisms are to be found in all. The present disputes are seemingly the result of one.—Nothing can be more undeniable than the supremacy of parliament over the most distant branches of the British empire: for although the king being esteemed, in the eye of the law, the original proprietor of all the lands in the kingdom; all lands, upon defect of heirs to succeed to an inheritance, escheat to the king; and all new discovered lands vest in him: yet in neither case can he exempt them from the jurisdiction of the legislature of the kingdom.

He may grant them, under leases or charters, to individuals or companies; with liberty of making rules and regulations for the internal government and improvement of them; but such regulations must ever be consistent with the laws of the kingdom, and subject to their controul.

On the other hand, I am extremely dubious, whether it be consistent with the general principles of liberty (with those of the British constitution, I think, it is not), to tax where there is no representation: the arguments hitherto adduced from Manchester and Birmingham, and other great towns, not having representatives, are foreign to the subject; at least they are by no means equal to it;—for every inhabitant, possessed of forty shillings freehold, has a vote in the election of members

INTRODUCTION.

bers for the county: but it is not the persons, but the property of men that is taxed, and there is not a foot of property in this kingdom, that is not represented.

It appears then, that certain principles exist in the British constitution, which militate with each other; the reason of their doing so is evident; it was never supposed that they would extend beyond the limits of Great Britain, or affect so distant a country as America. It is much to be wished, therefore, that some expedient could be thought of, to reconcile them.

The conduct of the several administrations, that have had the direction of the affairs of this kingdom, has been reciprocally arraigned; but, I think, without reason; for, all things considered, an impartial and dispassionate mind, will find many excuses to allege in justification of each.—The fewest, I am afraid, are to be pleaded in favour of the Americans, for they settled in America under charters, which expressly reserved to the British Parliament the authority, whether consistent or not consistent, now asserted. Although, therefore, they had a right to make humble representations to his majesty in parliament, and to shew the impropriety and inconvenience of inforcing such principles, yet they had certainly no right to oppose them.

Expedients may still be found, it is to be hoped however, to conciliate the present unhappy differences, and restore harmony again between Great Britain and her colonies; but whatever measures may be adopted by parliament, I am sure, it is

the

INTRODUCTION.

the duty and intereſt of America to ſubmit. — But it is impertinent to enter any further into the diſcuſſion of a ſubject, which is at this time under the deliberation of the moſt auguſt aſſembly in the world. I will, therefore, conclude with a ſincere prayer, that whatever meaſures may be adopted, they may be different in their iſſue, from what the fears of men generally lead them to preconceive; and that, if they be coercive ones, they may be inforced, which, I am perſuaded, is practicable, without the effuſion of a ſingle drop of blood: if lenient ones, which are preferable, and which I think equally practicable, without any loſs or diminution of the dignity or intereſt of this kingdom.

Greenwich,
Jan. 23d, 1775.

TRAVELS

THROUGH THE

MIDDLE SETTLEMENTS

IN

NORTH-AMERICA.

ON Friday the 27th of April 1759, I embarked, in company with several North-American gentlemen, on board the Difpatch, captain Necks, for Virginia; and the next day we fet fail from Spithead, under convoy of his majefty's fhip the Lynn, captain Sterling, commander, with thirty-three fail of trading veffels. We came to an anchor in the evening in Yarmouth Road, and the next day failed with a frefh eafterly wind through the Needles. *Anno 1*

We paffed by the Lizard, and in the evening difcovered a fail, which proved to be an Englifh floop laden with corn. She had been taken by a French privateer, and was making her way for France: there were three Frenchmen and one Englifhman on board. The commodore fent fome hands to her, with orders to carry her to Penzance. *April 3*

Thick, hazy weather with a fair wind. A large fhip paffed through the fleet about four o'clock in the afternoon: and in *May 1.*

the

the evening ancther veffel bore down upon the fternmoft fhips, and fpoke with them.

Fair, pleafant weather. The next day we found by our reckoning that we had made a hundred leagues from the Land's End.

Strong, violent gales at north and by weft. In the evening the Molly, captain Chew, had her main-top-maft carried away, and hoifted out a fignal of diftrefs.

From this time to the 14th, nothing remarkable happened: the wind was feldom fair; but the weather being moderate, we made frequent vifits, and paffed our time very agreeably.

Captain Necks fell ill of a fever, and continued indifpofed feveral days: he began to mend about the 17th.

In the afternoon, a fudden and violent fquall from the north-weft obliged us to lye-to under our reefed main-fail: it continued to increafe, and blew a ftorm for about thirty-fix hours, when it began to moderate.

We made fail in the forenoon, with about four fhips in company; and the next day in the evening were joined by eighteen more. From that time to the 28th, nothing remarkable happened: we had generally pleafant weather, but adverfe winds. We frequently vifited; and were much entertained with feeing grampufes, turtles, bonetas, porpoifes, flying and other fifh, common in the Atlantic.

We difcovered a large fail; fhe directed her courfe towards the eaft. We took her to be an Englifh man of war going exprefs. She carried three top-gallant fails.

We fpoke with a floop bound from Antigua to London. She acquainted the commodore with the agreeable news of his majefty's forces at Guadaloupe having reduced that whole ifland under fubjection to the Britifh government. The wind ftill continued unfavourable.

We

WILLIAMSBURG. VIRGINIA.

We spoke with a snow from Carolina, who informed the commodore, that a French frigate was cruising off the Capes of Virginia. From that time to the 11th, we had nothing remarkable. The wind was generally from west to north-west, and there were frequent squalls with lightning. We saw several bonetas, grampuses, albicores, and fish of different kinds. *1759. June 5.*

The water appeared discoloured; and we concluded that we were upon the Banks of Newfoundland: we cast the lead, but found no ground. The weather was thick and hazy. Nothing remarkable happened from this time to the 3d of July: we had pleasant weather, though now and then squalls with lightning. We fell in with several currents and had variable winds. *June 11.*

We had fine weather, with a gentle breeze at N. W. We were now, according to the commodore's reckoning (which we afterward found to be true), about sixty leagues from land. The air was richly scented with the fragrance of the pines. *July 3.*

We saw a great many sloops, from whence we imagined that we were near the coast. The wind was at east by north. *July 4.*

About six in the morning we caught some green fish: upon this we sounded, and found eighteen fathom water. At ten we discovered land, which proved to be Cape Charles; and about three hours afterward sailed through the capes into Chesapeak-Bay. The commodore took his leave to go upon a cruise; and at eight in the evening we came to an anchor in York-River, after a tedious and disagreeable voyage of almost ten weeks. *July 5.*

The next morning having hired a chaise at York, I went to Williamsburg, about twelve miles distant. The road is exceedingly pleasant, through some of the finest tobacco plantations in North-America, with a beautiful view of the river and woods of great extent.

WILLIAMSBURG. VIRGINIA.

Williamsburg is the capital of Virginia: it is situated between two creeks; one falling into James, the other into York River; and is built nearly due east and west. The distance of each landing-place is something more than a mile from the town; which, with the disadvantage of not being able to bring up large vessels, is the reason of its not having increased so fast as might have been expected. It consists of about two hundred houses, does not contain more than one thousand souls, whites and negroes; and is far from being a place of any consequence. It is regularly laid out in parallel streets, intersected by others at right angles; has a handsome square in the center, through which runs the principal street, one of the most spacious in North-America, three quarters of a mile in length, and above a hundred feet wide. At the ends of this street are two public buildings, the college and the capitol: and although the houses are of wood, covered with shingles, and but indifferently built, the whole makes a handsome appearance. There are few public edifices that deserve to be taken notice of: those, which I have mentioned, are the principal; and they are far from being magnificent. The governor's palace, indeed, is tolerably good, one of the best upon the continent; but the church, the prison, and the other buildings, are all of them extremely indifferent. The streets are not paved, and consequently very dusty, the soil hereabout consisting chiefly of sand: however, the situation of Williamsburg has one advantage, which few or no places in these lower parts have; that of being free from mosquitoes. Upon the whole, it is an agreeable residence; there are ten or twelve gentleman's families constantly residing in it, besides merchants and tradesmen. And at the times of the assemblies, and general courts, it is crowded with the gentry of the country: on those occasions there are balls and other amusements;

but

VIRGINIA.

but as foon as the bufinefs is finifhed, they return to their country houfes; and the town is in a manner deferted.

The fituation of Virginia (according to Evans's Map) is between the 36th and 40th degrees of north lat. and about 76 degrees weft long. from London. It is bounded on the north by the river Potowmac, on the eaft by the Atlantic Ocean, by Carolina on the fouth, and, to include only what is inhabited, by the great Alleghenny on the weft.

The climate is extremely fine, though fubject to violent heats in the fummer: Farenheit's thermometer being generally for three months from 85 to 95 degrees high. The other feafons, however, make ample amends for this inconvenience: for the autumns and fprings are delightful, and the winters fo mild and ferene (though there are now and then exceffive cold days) as fcarcely to require a fire. The only complaint that a perfon can reafonably make, is, of the very fudden changes which the weather is liable to; for this being intirely regulated by the winds, is exceedingly variable. Southerly winds are productive of heat, northerly of cold, and eafterly of rain; from hence it is no uncommon thing for the thermometer to fall many degrees in a very few hours; and, after a warm day, to have fuch fevere cold, as to freeze over a river a mile broad in one night's time*. In fummer there are frequent and violent gufts with thunder and lightning; but as the country is very thinly inhabited, and moft of the gentry have electrical rods to their houfes, they are not attended with many fatal accidents. Now and then, indeed, fome of the negroes lofe their lives; and

---

* On the 19th of December, 1759, being upon a vifit to colonel Wafhington, at Mount-Vernon, upon the river Potowmac, where it is two miles broad, I was greatly furprifed to find the river intirely frozen over in the fpace of one night, when the preceding day had been mild and temperate.

VIRGINIA.

it is not uncommon in the woods, to see trees torn and riven to pieces by their fury and violence. A remarkable circumstance happened some years ago at York, which is well attested: a person standing at his door during a thunder gust, was unfortunately killed; there was an intermediate tree at some distance, which was struck at the same time; and when they came to examine the body, they found the tree delineated upon it in miniature. Part of the body was livid, but that which was covered by the tree was of its natural colour.

I believe no country has more certainly proved the efficacy of electrical rods, than this: before the discovery of them, these gusts were frequently productive of melancholy consequences; but now it is rare to hear of such instances. It is observable that no house was ever struck, where they were fixed: and although it has frequently happened that the rods themselves have been melted, or broken to pieces, and the houses scorched along the sides of them, which manifested that they had received the stroke, but that the quantity of lightning was too great to be carried off by the conductor, yet never has any misfortune happened; such a direction having been given to the lightning, as to prevent any danger or ill consequence. These circumstances, one would imagine, should induce every person to get over those prejudices which many have entertained; and to consider the neglect, rather than the use of them as criminal, since they seem to be means put into our hands by Providence, for our safety and protection.

The soil of Virginia is in general good. There are indeed barrens where the lands produce nothing but pine-trees; but taking the whole tract together, it is certainly fertile. The low grounds upon the rivers and creeks are exceedingly rich, being loam intermingled with sand: and the higher you go up in the country, towards the mountains, the value of the land increases; for it grows more strong, and of a deeper clay.

Virginia, in its natural state, produces great quantities of fruits and medicinal plants, with trees and flowers of infinitely various kinds. Tobacco and Indian corn are the original produce of the country; likewise the pigeon-berry and rattlesnake-root, so esteemed in all ulcerous and pleuretical complaints: grapes, strawberries, hiccory nuts, mulberries, chesnuts, and several other fruits, grow wild and spontaneously.

Besides trees and flowers of an ordinary nature, the woods produce myrtles, cedars, cypresses, sugar trees, firs of different sorts, and no less than seven or eight kinds of oak; they are likewise adorned and beautified with red flowering maples, sassafras trees, dog-woods, acacias, red-buds, scarlet flowering chesnuts, fringe trees, flowering poplars, umbrellas, magnolias, yellow jasamines, chamœdaphnes, pacoons, atamusco lillies, May-apples, and innumerable other sorts; so that one may reasonably assert that no country ever appeared with greater elegance or beauty.

Not to notice too the almost numberless creeks and rivulets which every where abound, it is watered by four large rivers of such safe navigation, and such noble and majestic appearance, as not to be exceeded, perhaps, in the whole known world.

James river, which was formerly called Powhatan, from its having been the seat of that emperor, is seven miles broad at the mouth, navigable to the falls (above 150 miles) for vessels of large burden, and from thence to the mountains for small craft and canoes.

The falls are in length about six or seven miles; they consist of innumerable breaks of water, owing to the obstruction of the current by an infinite number of rocks, which are scattered over the bed of the river; and form a most picturesque and beautiful cascade.

The

VIRGINIA.

The honourable colonel Byrd has a small place called Belvedere, upon a hill at the lower end of these falls, as romantic and elegant as any thing I have ever seen. It is situated very high, and commands a fine prospect of the river, which is half a mile broad, forming cataracts in the manner above described; there are several little islands scattered carelessly about, very rocky, and covered with trees; and two or three villages in view at a small distance. Over all these you discover a prodigious extent of wilderness, and the river winding majestically along through the midst of it.

York river, for about forty miles, to a place called West Point, is confined in one channel about two miles broad: it flows in a very direct course, making but one angle, and that an inconsiderable one, during the whole way. At West Point it forks, and divides itself into two branches; the southward called Pamunky; the northward Mattapony: each of these branches, including the windings and meanders of the river, is navigable seventy or eighty miles, and a considerable way of this space for large ships.

The Rappahannoc is navigable to the falls, which are a mile above Fredericsburg, and about 110 from the bay. Vessels of large burden may come up to this place; and small craft and canoes may be carried up much higher.

The Potowmac is one of the finest rivers in North America: it is ten miles broad at the mouth, navigable above 200 miles, to Alexandria, for men of war, and, allowing for a few carrying places, for canoes above 200 farther, to the very branches of the Ohio. Colonel Boquet, a Swiss gentleman in the Royal Americans, came down this autumn from Fort Cumberland * to Shenando with very little difficulty; from hence to the great

---

* From Fort Cumberland to Shenando is above 100 miles; from Shenando to the great falls about 60; and from the great falls to Alexandria about 17 or 18.

VIRGINIA.

falls, I have been told, a navigation may eafily be effected. So that this river feems to promife to be of as great confequence as any in North America.

In all thefe rivers the tide flows as far as the falls, and at Alexandria it rifes between two and three feet. They difcharge themfelves into Chefapeak Bay, one of the fineft in the world, which runs a great way up the country into Maryland; is from ten to twenty miles broad; navigable near a hundred leagues for veffels of almoft any burden; and receives into its bofom at leaft twenty great rivers.

Thefe waters are ftored with incredible quantities of fifh, fuch as fheeps-heads, rock-fifh, drums, white pearch, herrings, oyfters, crabs, and feveral other forts. Sturgeon and fhad are in fuch prodigious numbers, that one day, within the fpace of two miles only, fome gentlemen in canoes caught above 600 of the former with hooks, which they let down to the bottom, and drew up at a venture when they perceived them to rub againft a fifh; and of the latter above 5000 have been caught at one fingle haul of the feine.

In the mountains there are very rich veins of ore; fome mines having been already opened which turn to great account; particularly Spotfwood's iron mine upon the Rappahannoc, out of which they melt annually above fix hundred ton: and one of copper upon the Roanoke, belonging to colonel Chifwell. This laft mentioned gentleman is alfo going to try for lead upon fome hunting grounds belonging to the Indians, towards New River, and the Green Briar; where, it is faid, there is fine ore, and in great plenty, lying above ground. Some coal mines have alfo been opened upon James River near the falls, which are likely to anfwer very well.

The forefts abound with plenty of game of various kinds; hares, turkies, pheafants, woodcocks, and partridges, are in

VIRGINIA.

the greatest abundance. In the marshes are found sorufes, a particular species of bird, more exquisitely delicious than the ortolan, snipes also and ducks of various kinds. The American shell-drake and bluewing exceed all of the duck kind whatsoever; and these are in prodigious numbers. In the woods there are variety of birds remarkable both for singing and for beauty; of which are the mocking-bird, the red-bird or nightingale, the blue-bird, the yellow-bird, the humming-bird*, the Baltimore-bird, the summer-duck, the turtle, and several other sorts.

Reptiles and insects are almost innumerable: some of them, indeed are harmless and beautiful; such as the black-snake, the bead-snake, the garter-snake, the fire-fly, and several sorts of butterflies; but the rattle-snake and viper, and many others are exceedingly venomous and deadly †. Of quadrupeds there are various kinds; squirrels of four or five different species ‡,

---

* The humming-bird is the smallest and the most beautiful of all the feathered race: its colours are green, crimson, and gold: it lives chiefly by suction upon the sweets and essences of flowers: and nothing can be more curious than to observe numbers of them in gardens where there are honeysuckles or trumpet-flowers, flying from flower to flower, putting their slender bills into every one, and sucking out the sweetest juices. The motion of their wings is incredibly swift, and produces a humming noise, not unlike that of a large humble bee. They are frequently kept in cages, but seldom live longer than two months. The food which is given them, is either honey or sugar, mixed with water. Repeated attempts have been made to send them alive to England, but always without success.

† There are two very curious species of frogs in Virginia; one is called the bull-frog, which is prodigiously large, and makes so loud a noise, that it may be heard at a great distance: the other is a small green frog, which sits upon the boughs of trees, and is found in almost every garden.

See Catesby's Natural History of Carolina.

‡ Of the several species of squirrels, the ground and flying-squirrels are much the smallest and most beautiful. The former are of a dusky orange hue,

opof-

VIRGINIA.

opoffums, racoons, foxes, beavers, and deer: and in the defarts and uninhabited parts, wolves, bears, panthers, elks or moofe-deer, buffaloes, mountain-cats, and various other forts. Such are in general the natural productions of this country.

Viewed and confidered as a fettlement, Virginia is far from being arrived at that degree of perfection which it is capable of. Not a tenth of the land is yet cultivated: and that which is cultivated, is far from being fo in the moft advantageous manner. It produces, however, confiderable quantities of grain and cattle and fruit of many kinds. The Virginian pork is faid to be fuperior in flavour to any in the world; but the fheep and horned cattle being fmall and lean, the meat of them is inferior to that of Great Britain, or indeed, of moft parts of Europe. The horfes are fleet and beautiful; and the gentlemen of Virginia, who are exceedingly fond of horfe-racing, have fpared no expence or trouble to improve the breed of them by importing great numbers from England.

The fruits introduced here from Europe fucceed extremely well; particularly peaches, which have a very fine flavour, and grow in fuch plenty as to ferve to feed the hogs in the autumn of the year. Their bloffoms in the fpring make a beautiful appearance throughout the country.

---

ftreaked with black; the latter grey or afh-coloured, and elegantly formed. Thefe have a fpreading or fan-tail, and two membranes adhering to their fides; which when they fpring or leap from a tree, they expand, and are thereby enabled to fly through a confiderable fpace. The former are of a very wild nature; but thefe may be eafily, and are frequently tamed.—There is a fpecies of polecat in this part of America, which is commonly called a fkunk. This animal, when purfued, or affailed by its enemy, ejects its urine; which emits fuch a fetid and infupportable ftench, as almoft to ftifle and fuffocate whatever is within the reach of it.

Virginia is divided into fifty-two counties, and feventy-feven parifhes, and by act of affembly there ought to be forty-four towns; but one half of thefe have not more than five houfes; and the other half are little better than inconfiderable villages. This is owing to the cheapnefs of land, and the commodioufnefs of navigation: for every perfon may with eafe procure a fmall plantation, can fhip his tobacco at his own door, and live independent. When the colony fhall come to be more thickly feated, and land grow dear, people will be obliged to follow trades and manufactures, which will neceffarily make towns and large cities; but this feems remote, and not likely to happen for fome centuries.

The inhabitants are fuppofed to be in number between two and three hundred thoufand. There are a hundred and five thoufand titheables, under which denomination are included all white males from fixteen to fixty; and all negroes whatfoever within the fame age. The former are obliged to ferve in the militia, and amount to forty thoufand.

The trade of this colony is large and extenfive. Tobacco is the principal article of it. Of this they export annually between fifty and fixty thoufand hogfheads, each hogfhead weighing eight hundred or a thoufand weight: fome years they export much more. They fhip alfo for the Madeiras, the Streights, and the Weft-Indies, feveral articles, fuch as grain, pork, lumber, and cyder: to Great Britain, bar-iron, indigo, and a fmall quantity of ginfeng, though of an inferior quality; and they clear out one year with another about
ton of fhipping.

Their manufactures are very inconfiderable. They make a kind of cotton-cloth, with which they clothe themfelves in common, and call after the name of their country; and fome inconsiderable quantities of linen, hose, and other trifling articles: but nothing to deserve attention.

The government is a royal one: the legislature, consisting of a governor appointed by the king; a council of twelve persons, under the same nomination; and a house of burgesses, or representatives, of a hundred and eight or ten members, elected by the people; two for each county, and one for each of the following places, viz. the College of William and Mary, James-town, Norfolk-borough, and Williamsburg. Each branch has a negative.—All laws in order to be permanent, must have the king's approbation; nor must any be enacted, which may be repugnant to the laws of Great Britain.

The courts of judicature are either county, or general courts. The county courts are held monthly in each county, at a place assigned for that purpose, by the justices thereof: four of them making a quorum. They are appointed by the governor, and take cognizance of all causes, at common law, or in chancery, within their respective counties, except criminal ones, punishable with loss of life, or member. This power they are not permitted to exercise except over negroes and slaves, and then not without a special commission from the governor for each particular purpose*. The general court is held twice a year

---

* How necessary it may be that they should have such a power, even in this case, I will not pretend to say? but the law which transfers it to them seems so inconsistent with the natural rights of mankind, that I cannot but in pity to humanity recite it.

" Every slave committing any offence, by law punishable by death, or loss
" of member, shall be committed to the county goal, and the sheriff of the
" county shall forthwith certify such commitment, with the cause thereof,
" to the governor, or commander in chief, who may issue a commission of
" oyer and terminer to such persons as he shall think fit, which persons, forth-
" with after the receipt of such commission, shall cause the offender to be

VIRGINIA.

at Williamsburg. It consists of the governor and council, any five of which make a court. They hear and determine all causes whatsoever, ecclesiastical, or civil, and sit four and twenty days: the first five of these are for hearing and determining suits in chancery appeals from the decrees of the county or inferior courts in chancery; and writs of superfedeas to such decrees. The other days are for trying suits or prosecutions in behalf of the king; and all other matters depending in the said court. Appeals are allowed to the king in council, in cases of 500 l. sterling value. The governor has a power of pardoning criminals in all cases, except of treason or murder. And then he can only reprieve till he knows the king's pleasure.

The established religion is that of the church of England; and there are very few Dissenters of any denomination in this province. There are at present between sixty and seventy clergymen; men in general of sober and exemplary lives. They have each a glebe of two or three hundred acres of land, a house, and a salary established by law of 16,000 weight of tobacco, with an allowance of 1700 more for shrinkage. This is delivered to them in hogsheads ready packed for exportation, at the most convenient warehouse. The presentation of livings is in the hands of the vestry; which is a standing body of twelve members, invested with the sole power of raising levies, settling the repairs of the church, and regulating other

---

" publicly arraigned and tried at the court-house of the said county, and take
" for evidence the confession of the offender, the oath of one or more credi-
" ble witnesses, or such testimony of negroes, mulattoes, or Indians, bond
" or free, with pregnant circumstances as to them shall seem convincing,
" *without the solemnity of a jury*, and the offender being found guilty, shall
" pass such judgment upon him or her as the law directs for the like crimes,
" and on such judgment award execution."
Mercer's Abridgment of the Virginian Laws, p. 342.

parochial bufinefs. They were originally elected by the people of the feveral parifhes; but now fill up vacancies themfelves. If the veftry does not prefent to a living in lefs than twelve months, it lapfes to the governor. The diocefan is the bifhop of London; who has a power of appointing a commiffary to prefide over, and convene the clergy on particular occafions; and to cenfure, or even fufpend them, in cafes of neglect or immorality. His falary is 100 l. fterling per annum; and he is generally of the council, which is of equal emolument to him *.

An unhappy difagreement has lately arifen between the clergy and the laity, which, it is to be feared, may be of ferious confequence. The caufe of it was this. Tobacco being extremely fcarce from a general failure of the crop, the affembly paffed an act to oblige the clergy and all public officers to receive their ftipends in money inftead of tobacco. This the clergy remonftrated againft, alledging the hardfhip of being obliged to take a fmall price for their tobacco, when it bore an extravagant one; feeing they never had any kind of compenfation allowed, when it was fo plentiful as to be almoft a drug. They fent over an agent to England, and the law was repealed. This greatly exafperated the people; and fuch is their mutual animofity at this time, that, I fear, it will not eafily fubfide, or be forgotten.

With regard to the law in queftion, it was certainly a very hard one; and I doubt whether, upon principles of free government, it can be defended; or whether the affembly can legally interpofe any farther, than, in cafes of neceffity, to oblige the clergy to receive their falaries in money inftead of to-

---

* The commiffary is commonly prefident of the college, and has the parifh of Williamfburg, or fome other lucrative parifh, which render him about 350l. a year: fo that his annual income is between 5 and 600l.

bacco,

bacco, at the current price of tobacco. They may, I am perfuaded, in cafes of exigency, always make, and might then have made, fuch a law, without any confiderable detriment to the colony: for, fuppofing the price of tobacco to be, what it was at that time, about fifty fhillings currency per hundred, what would the whole fum be, were the clergy to be paid ad valorem? Not 20000l. fterling. There are in Virginia, as I obferved before, about fixty-five clergymen: each of thefe is allowed 16,000 weight of tobacco; which, at the rate of fifty fhillings currency per hundred, amounts to 400l.; 400l. multiplied by 65, is equal to 26,000 l.; which, allowing 40 per cent. difcount, the difference of exchange, is about 18571 l. fterling. Now what is this fum to fuch a colony as Virginia? But to this it will be faid, perhaps, why fhould the clergy be gainers in a time of public diftrefs, when every one elfe is a fufferer? The clergy will doubtlefs reply, and why fhould the clergy be the only fufferers in plentiful feafons, when all but themfelves are gainers? Upon the whole, however, as on the one hand I difapprove of the proceedings of the affembly in this affair, fo, on the other, I cannot approve of the fteps which were taken by the clergy. That violence of temper; that indecent behaviour towards the governor; that unworthy treatment of their commiffary; and, to mention nothing elfe, that confufion of proceeding in the convention, of which fome, though not the majority, as has been invidioufly reprefented, were guilty; thefe things were furely unbecoming the facred character they are invefted with; and the moderation of thofe perfons, who ought in all things to imitate the conduct of their divine Mafter. If, inftead of flying out in invectives againft the legiflature; of accufing the governor of having given up the caufe of religion by paffing the bill; when, in fact, had he rejected it, he would never have been able to have got any fupplies

plies during the courſe of the war, though ever ſo much wanted; if, inſtead of charging the commiſſary with want of zeal for having exhorted them to moderate meaſures, they had followed the prudent counſels of that excellent man, and had acted with more temper and moderation, they might, I am perſuaded, in a very ſhort time, have obtained any redreſs they could reaſonably have deſired. The people in general were extremely well affected towards the clergy, and had ſhewn their regard for them in ſeveral inſtances; they were ſenſible, moreover, that their ſalaries were too ſcanty to ſupport them with dignity, and there had been ſome talk about raiſing them: had the clergy, therefore, before they applied to England, only offered a memorial to the aſſembly, ſetting forth that they thought the act extremely hard upon them, as their ſalaries were ſmall; and that they hoped the aſſembly would take their caſe into conſideration, and enable them to live with that dignity which became their character; I am perſuaded from the knowledge which I have of the people in general, and from repeated converſations with ſeveral members of the aſſembly, that they might have obtained almoſt any thing they could have wiſhed; if not, they undoubtedly would have had reaſon to appeal. But inſtead of this, without applying to the aſſembly for relief, after the act was paſſed, (for before, indeed, ſome of them did apply to the ſpeaker in private) they flew out into the moſt violent invectives, immediately ſent over an agent to England, and appealed to his majeſty in council. The reſult has been already related.

The progreſs of arts and ſciences in this colony has been very inconſiderable: the college of William and Mary is the only public place of education, and this has by no means anſwered the deſign of its inſtitution. It has a foundation for a preſident and ſix profeſſors. The buſineſs of the preſident is to ſuper-

1759.
superintend the whole, and to read four theological lectures annually. He has a handsome house to live in, and 200l. sterling per annum. The professor of the Indian school has 60l. sterling, and a house also; his business is to instruct the Indians in reading, writing, and the principles of the Christian religion: this pious institution was set on foot and promoted by the excellent Mr. Boyle. The professor of humanity has the care of instructing the students in classical learning: he has an usher or assistant under him. The four other professors teach moral philosophy, metaphysics, mathematics, and divinity. Each of the professors has apartments in the college, and a salary of about 80 l. per annum *. The present chancellor of the college is the bishop of London.

From what has been said of this colony, it will not be difficult to form an idea of the character † of its inhabitants. The climate and external appearance of the country conspire to make them indolent, easy, and good-natured; extremely fond of society, and much given to convivial pleasures. In consequence of this, they seldom show any spirit of enterprize, or expose themselves willingly to fatigue. Their authority over their slaves renders them vain and imperious, and entire strangers to that elegance of sentiment, which is so peculiarly characteristic of refined and polished nations. Their ignorance of mankind and of learning, exposes them to many errors and prejudices, especially in regard to Indians and Negroes, whom they scarcely consider as of the human species; so that it is almost impossible, in cases of violence, or even murder, committed upon those unhappy people by any of the planters, to have the delinquents brought to justice. For either the

* They have been since raised, I believe, to 100l.
† General characters are always liable to many exceptions. In Virginia I have had the pleasure to know several gentlemen adorned with many virtues and accomplishments, to whom the following description is by no means applicable.

grand

VIRGINIA.

grand jury refuse to find the bill, or the petit jury bring in their verdict, not guilty *.

The display of a character thus constituted, will naturally be in acts of extravagance, ostentation, and a disregard of œconomy; it is not extraordinary, therefore, that the Virginians outrun their incomes; and that having involved themselves in difficulties, they are frequently tempted to raise money by bills of exchange, which they know will be returned protested, with 10 per cent. interest †.

---

* There are two laws in this colony, which make it almost impossible to convict a planter, or white man, of the death of a Negroe or Indian. By the first it is enacted, that "if any slave shall die by reason of any stroke or blow, given in correction by his or her owner, or by reason of any accidental blow whatsoever, given by such owner; no person concerned in such correction, or accidental homicide, shall undergo any prosecution or punishment for the same; unless, upon examination before the county court, it shall be proved by the oath of one lawful and credible witness, at least, that such slave was killed wilfully, maliciously, and designedly; nor shall any person indicted for the murder of a slave, and upon trial found guilty only of manslaughter, incur any forfeiture or punishment for such offence or misfortune." See Mercer's Abridgment, p. 345. By the second, "No Negro, Mulatto, or Indian, can be admitted in any court, or before any migistrate, to be sworn as a witness, or give evidence in any cause whatsoever, except upon the trial of a slave for a capital offence. Mercer's Abridgment, p. 419.

† By an act of assembly, if any bill of exchange is drawn for the payment of any sum of money, and such bill is protested for non-acceptance or non-payment, it carries interest from the date thereof, after the rate of 10 per cent. per annum, until the money be fully satisfied and paid.

A very curious anecdote relative to this law was mentioned to me at Williamsburg, of which I am persuaded the reader will excuse the relation.—An usurer, not satisfied with 5l. per cent. legal interest, refused to advance a sum of money to a gentleman, unless, by way of security, he would give him a bill of exchange that should be returned protested, by which he would be entitled to 10 per cent. The gentleman, who had immediate occasion for the money, sat down and drew a bill upon a capital merchant in London, with whom he

VIRGINIA.

1759.

The public or political character of the Virginians, correfponds with their private one : they are haughty and jealous of their liberties, impatient of reftraint, and can fcarcely bear the thought of being controuled by any fuperior power. Many of them confider the colonies as independent ftates, unconnected with Great Britain, otherwife than by having the fame common king, and being bound to her with natural affection. There are but few of them that have a turn for bufinefs, and even thofe are by no means expert at it. I have known them, upon a very urgent occafion, vote the relief of a garrifon, without once confidering whether the thing was practicable, when it was moft evidently and demonftrably otherwife *. In

had never had any tranfaction, or carried on the leaft correfpondence. The merchant, on the receipt of the bill, obferving the name of the drawer, very readily honoured it, knowing the gentleman to be a perfon of great property, and concluding that he meant to enter into correfpondence with him. The ufurer upon this became entitled to only 5l. per cent. He was exceedingly enraged, therefore, at being as he fuppofed thus tricked : and complained very heavily to the gentleman of his having given him a good bill inftead of a bad one.

* The garrifon here alluded to, was that of Fort Loudoun, in the Cherokee country, confifting of a lieutenant and about fifty men. This unfortunate party being befieged by the Cherokee Indians, and reduced to the laft extremity, fent off runners to the governors of Virginia and Carolina, imploring immediate fuccour ; adding that it was impoffible for them to hold out above twenty days longer. The affembly of Virginia, commiferating their unhappy fituation, very readily voted a confiderable fum for their relief. With this, troops were to be levied ; were to rendezvous upon the frontiers 200 miles diftant from Williamfburg ; were afterwards to proceed to the fort 200 miles farther through a wildernefs, where there was no road, no magazines, no pofts, either to fhelter the fick, or cover a retreat in cafe of any difafter ; fo that the unfortunate garrifon might as effectually have been fuccoured from the moon. The author taking notice of thefe difficulties to one of the members, he frankly replied, " Faith, it is true : but " we have had an opportunity at leaft of fhowing our loyalty." In a few days after arrived the melancholy news, that this unfortunate party was entirely cut off.

mat-

VIRGINIA.

matters of commerce they are ignorant of the neceſſary principles that muſt prevail between a colony and its mother-country; they think it a hardſhip not to have an unlimited trade to every part of the world. They conſider the duties upon their ſtaple as injurious only to themſelves; and it is utterly impoſſible to perſuade them that they affect the conſumer alſo. Upon the whole, however, to do them juſtice, the ſame ſpirit of generoſity prevails here which does in their private character; they never refuſe any neceſſary ſupplies for the ſupport of government when called upon, and are a generous and loyal people.

The women are, upon the whole, rather handſome, though not to be compared with our fair country-women in England. They have but few advantages, and conſequently are ſeldom accompliſhed: this makes them reſerved, and unequal to any intereſting or refined converſation. They are immoderately fond of dancing, and indeed it is almoſt the only amuſement they partake of: but even in this they diſcover great want of taſte and elegance, and ſeldom appear with that gracefulneſs and eaſe, which theſe movements are ſo calculated to diſplay. Towards the cloſe of an evening, when the company are pretty well tired with country dances, it is uſual to dance jiggs; a practice originally borrowed, I am informed, from the * Negroes. Theſe dances are without any method or regularity: a gentleman and lady ſtand up, and dance about the room, one of them retiring, the other purſuing, then perhaps meeting, in an irregular fantaſtical manner. After ſome time, another lady gets up, and then the firſt lady muſt ſit down, ſhe being, as they term it, cut out: the ſecond lady acts the ſame

---

* The author has ſince had an opportunity of obſerving ſomething ſimilar in Italy. The treſcone of the Tuſcans is very like the jiggs of the Virginians.

VIRGINIA.

part which the first did, till somebody cuts her out. The genmen perform in the same manner. The Virginian ladies, excepting these amusements chiefly spend their time in sewing and taking care of their families : they seldom read, or endeavour to improve their minds ; however, they are in general good housewives ; and though they have not, I think, quite so much tenderness and sensibility as the English ladies ; yet they make as good wives, and as good mothers, as any in the world.

It is hard to determine whether this colony can be called flourishing, or not : because, though it produces great quantities of tobacco and grain, yet there seem to be very few improvements carrying on it. Great part of Virginia is a wilderness, and as many of the gentlemen are in possession of prodigious tracts of land, it is likely to continue so. A spirit of enterprize is by no means the turn of the colony, and therefore few attempts have been made to force a trade; which I think might easily be done, both to the West-Indies and the Ohio. They have every thing necessary for such an undertaking, viz. lumber, provisions, grain, and every other commodity, which the other colonies, that subsist and grow rich by these means, make use of for exports ; but, instead of this, they have only a trifling communication with the West-Indies ; and as to the Ohio, they have suffered themselves, notwithstanding the superior advantages they might enjoy from having a water-carriage almost to the Yoghiogheny, to neglect this valuable branch of commerce ; while the industrious Pensylvanians seize every opportunity, and struggle with innumerable difficulties, to secure it to themselves. The Virginians are content, if they can but live from hand to mouth ; they confine themselves almost intirely to the cultivation of tobacco ; and if they have but enough of this to pay their merchants in London, and to provide for
their

their pleasures; they are satisfied, and desire nothing more. Some few, indeed, have been rather more enterprising, and have endeavoured to improve their estates by raising indigo, and other schemes: but whether it has been owing to the climate, to their inexperience in these matters, or their want of perseverance, I am unable to determine, but their success has not answered their expectations.

The taxes of this colony are considerable, and the public debt amounts to at least 400,000 l. currency; this they have been driven into by the war, having seldom had less than a thousand or fifteen hundred provincial troops in pay, exclusive of the expences of some forts. The ways and means employed for raising the money, have been generally the same: they have first made an emission of so much paper currency as the exigency required, and then laid a tax for sinking it. This tax has been commonly upon lands and negroes, two shillings for every titheable; and a shilling or eighteen pence upon every hundred acres of land. This mode of taxation has occasioned some divisions in the house; for the owners of large tracts, being unable, perhaps, to cultivate a tenth part of their possessions, and every man's real income arising from the number of his negroes, have thought it very hard to pay a tax for what they pretend is of no value to them: but much better arguments may be urged in support of the tax than against it.

The taxes for the present debt are laid till the year sixty-nine, when the whole, if they add nothing more to it, will be discharged. The use of paper-currency in this colony has intirely banished from it gold and silver. Indeed the introduction of it was certain in time to produce this effect; but left it should not, the Virginians fell into a measure, which completed it at once: for by an act of assembly they fixed the exchange between currency and sterling debts at five and twenty per cent.

not

not considering that the real value of their currency could only be regulated by itself. The consequence was, that when from frequent emissions, the difference of exchange between bills upon merchants in London and currency, was at 40 per cent. the difference between currency and specie * was only five and twenty. So that the monied men collected all the specie they could, sent it away to Philadelphia, where it passed for its real value, purchased bills of exchange with it there, and sold them again in Virginia with fifteen per cent. profit. And this they continued to do till there was not a pistole or a dollar remaining.

During my stay in Virginia, I made several excursions into different parts of the country: one in particular to the great falls of Potowmac; of which, as I expected to be highly entertained, I kept a journal.

I departed from Williamsburg, Oct. 1, 1759, in company with another gentleman; and we travelled that day about forty miles, to a plantation in king William-County; beautifully situated upon a high hill, on the north side of Pamunky river. A little below this place stands the Pamunky Indian town; where at present are the few remains of that large tribe; the rest having dwindled away through intemperance and disease. They live in little wigwams or cabins upon the river; and have a very fine tract of land of about 2000 acres, which they are restrained from alienating by act of assembly. Their employment is chiefly hunting or fishing, for the neighbouring gentry. They commonly dress like the Virginians, and I have sometimes mistaken them for the lower sort of that people. The night I spent here, they went out into an adjoining marsh to catch sorufes; and one of them, as I was informed in the

---

* Fixing the difference between currency and sterling debts, was, in reality, fixing it between currency and specie.

morning, caught near a hundred dozen. The manner of taking these birds is remarkable. The forus is not known to be in Virginia, except for about six weeks from the latter end of September: at that time they are found in the marshes in prodigious numbers, feeding upon the wild oats. At first they are exceedingly lean, but in a short time grow so fat, as to be unable to fly: in this state they lie upon the reeds, and the Indians go out in canoes and knock them on the head with their paddles. They are rather bigger than a lark, and are delicious eating. During the time of their continuing in season, you meet with them at the tables of most of the planters, breakfast, dinner, and supper*.

Oct. 2. We went to another plantation about twenty-four miles distant, belonging to a private gentleman upon Mattapony river. We staid there all that and the next day on account of rain.

Oct. 4. We travelled twenty-five miles to another gentleman's house; and from thence, the day following, about twenty-five miles farther, to a town called Fredericsburg.

Fredericsburg is situated about a mile below the Falls of Rappahannoc: it is regularly laid out, as most of the towns in Virginia are, in parallel streets. Part of it is built upon an eminence, and commands a delightful prospect; the rest upon the edge of the water for the convenience of warehouses. The town was begun about thirty-two years ago, for the sake of car-

---

* In several parts of Virginia the ancient custom of eating meat at breakfast still continues. At the top of the table, where the lady of the house presides, there is constantly tea and coffee; but the rest of the table is garnished out with roast fowls, ham, venison, game, and other dainties. Even at Williamsburg, it is the custom to have a plate of cold ham upon the table; and there is scarcely a Virginian lady who breakfasts without it.

E rying

rying on a trade with the back-settlers; and is at present by far the most flourishing one in these parts.

We left Fredericsburg the 6th instant, and went to see the Falls. At this place is a small mercantile town called Falmouth; whose inhabitants are endeavouring to rival the Fredericsburghers in their trade. It is built upon the north-side of the river, and consists of eighteen or twenty houses.

The Falls of Rappahannoc are similar to those of James river, except that they are not upon so large a scale. The whole range scarcely exceeds half a mile, and the breadth not a hundred yards. At the time of our going to see them, there was a fresh in the river, which added very much to their beauty. The center of view was an island of about a hundred acres covered with trees: this divided the river into two branches, in each of which, at regular distances of fifteen or twenty yards, was a chain of six or seven falls, one above another, the least of them a foot perpendicular. The margin was beautifully variegated with rocks and trees, and the whole formed a pleasing romantic scene.

At this place we met with a person who informed us of his having been, a few days before, a spectator of that extraordinary phenomenon in nature, the fascinating power of the rattle-snake. He observed one lying coiled near a tree, looking directly at a bird which had settled there. The bird was under great agitation, uttered the most doleful cries, hopped from spray to spray, and at length flew directly down to the snake, which opened its mouth and swallowed it.

From hence we ascended up the river, about fifteen miles, to Spotswood's iron-mines; and in our way had a fine view of the Apalachian mountains, or Blue Ridge, at the distance of seventy miles. At this place I was much affected with the following incident. A gentleman in our company, which was

now

now increafed, had a fmall negro boy with him, about fourteen years of age, that had lived with him in a remote part of the country fome time as a fervant; an old woman who was working in the mines, and who proved to be the boy's grandmother, accidentally caft her eyes on him; fhe viewed him with great attention for fome time; then fcreamed out, faying that it was her child, and flung herfelf down upon the ground. She lay there fome feconds; rofe up, looked on him again in an extafy of joy, and fell upon his neck and kiffed him. After this, fhe retired a few paces, examined him afrefh with fixed attention, and immediately feemed to lofe herfelf in thoughtful and profound melancholy. The boy all this while ftood filent and motionlefs; reclining his head on one fide, pale and affected beyond defcription. Upon the whole, it would not have been in the power of Raphael, to have imagined a finer picture of diftrefs.

We returned from this place the next day to Fredericfburg; and ferrying over the Rappahannoc into the Northern Neck, travelled about feventeen miles to a gentleman's houfe in Stafford County: in the morning we proceeded through Dumfries, and over Occoquan river to Colchefter, about twenty-one miles.

Thefe are two fmall towns lately built for the fake of the back trade; the former on Acquia creek, the other upon Occoquan river, both of which fall into the Potowmac. About two miles above Colchefter there is an iron furnace, a forge, two fawmills, and a bolting-mill: at our return we had an opportunity of vifiting them: they have every convenience of wood and water, that can be wifhed for. The ore wrought here is brought from Maryland; not that there is any doubt of there being plenty enough in the adjacent hills; but the inhabitants are difcouraged from trying for it by the proprietor's (viz. lord

MOUNT VERNON.

Fairfax) having reserved to himself a third of all ore that may be discovered in the Northern Neck. From Colchester we went about twelve miles farther to Mount Vernon. This place is the property of colonel Washington, and truly deserving of its owner *. The house is most beautifully situated upon a very high hill on the banks of the Potowmac; and commands a noble prospect of water, of cliffs, of woods and plantations. The river is near two miles broad, though two hundred from the mouth; and divides the dominion of Virginia from Maryland †. We rested here one day, and proceeded up the river

* I cannot omit this opportunity of bearing testimony to the gallant and public spirit of this gentleman. Nov. 1, 1753, Lieut. Gov. Dinwiddie having informed the assembly of Virginia, that the French had erected a fort upon the Ohio, it was resolved to send somebody to M. St. Pierre the commander, to claim that country as belonging to his Britannic majesty, and to order him to withdraw. Mr. Washington, a young gentleman of fortune just arrived at age, offered his service on this important occasion. The distance was more than 400 miles; 200 of which lay through a trackless desart, inhabited by cruel and merciless savages; and the season was uncommonly severe. Notwithstanding these discouraging circumstances, Mr. Washington, attended by one companion only, set out upon this dangerous enterprize: travelled from Winchester on foot, carrying his provisions on his back, executed his commission; and after incredible hardships, and many providential escapes, returned safe to Williamsburg, and gave an account of his negociation to the assembly, the 14th day of February following.

† A very curious fight is frequently exhibited upon this and the other great rivers in Virginia, which for its novelty is exceedingly diverting to strangers. During the spring and summer months the fishing-hawk is often seen hovering over the rivers, or resting on the wing without the least visible change of place for some minutes, then suddenly darting down and plunging into the water, from whence it seldom rises again without a rock fish, or some other considerable fish in its talons. It immediately shakes off the water like a mist, and makes the best of its way towards the woods. The bald-eagle, which is generally upon the watch, instantly pursues, and if it can overtake, endeavours to soar above it. The hawk grown follicitous for its own safety drops the

FALLS OF POTOWMAC.

about twenty-six miles to take a view of the Great Falls. These are formed in some respect like those of the Rappahannoc; but are infinitely more noble. The channel of the river is contracted by hills, and is as narrow, I was told, as at Fort Cumberland, which is an hundred and fifty miles higher up. It is clogged moreover with innumerable rocks; so that the water for a mile or two flows with accelerated velocity. At length coming to a ledge of rocks, which runs diametrically cross the river, it divides into two spouts, each about eight yards wide, and rushes down a precipice with incredible rapidity. The spout on the Virginian side makes three falls, one above another; the first about ten feet, the next fifteen, and the last twenty-four or twenty-five feet perpendicular. The water is of a vast bulk, and almost intire; the spout on the Maryland side is nearly equal in height and quantity, but a great deal more broken. These two spouts, after running in separate channels for a short space, at length unite in one about thirty yards wide; and as we judged from the smoothness of the surface and our unsuccessful endeavours to fathom it, of prodigious depth. The rocks on each side are at least ninety or a hundred feet high; and yet in great freshes, the water overflows the tops of them, as appeared by several large and intire trees, which had lodged there.

In the evening we returned down the river about sixteen miles to Alexandria, or Bel-haven, a small trading place in one of the finest situations imaginable. The Potowmac above and below the town, is not more than a mile broad, but it here opens into a large circular bay, of at least twice that diameter.

The town is built upon an arc of this bay; at one extremity of which is a wharf; at the other a dock for building

fish, and the bald-eagle never fails to stoop and catch it in its pounces before it reaches the water, leaving the hawk to go and fish for another.

ships;

ships; with water sufficiently deep to launch a vessel of any rate or magnitude.

The next day we returned to colonel Washington's, and in a few days afterward to Williamsburg.

The time of my residence in this colony was ten months, and I received so many instances of friendship and good-nature, that not to acknowledge them would be an act of ingratitude. It would not be easy to mention particular instances, without being guilty of injustice by omitting others. But, in general, I can truly affirm, that I took leave of this hospitable people with regret, and shall ever remember them with gratitude and affection.

1760. May 26. Having procured three horses, for myself, servant, and baggage, I departed from Williamsburg, and travelled that night to Eltham; twenty-five miles.

May 27. I ferried over Pamunky river at Danfies, and went to Todd's ordinary upon Mattopony, or the northern branch of York river; thirty-two miles.

May 28. I went to a plantation in Caroline county; twenty-seven miles.

May 29. To Fredericsburg; twenty-five miles.

As I was travelling this day, I observed a large black-snake, about six feet long, lying cross the stump of a tree by the road side. I touched it with my switch several times before it stirred; at last it darted with incredible swiftness into the woods. On my looking into the hole, where it had fixed its head, I observed a small bead-snake about two feet long; beautifully variegated with red, black, and orange colour, which the black-snake was watching to prey upon. I took and laid it, half stupified, in the sun to revive. After I had proceeded about a quarter of a mile, it occurred to me that it would be a great curiosity if I could carry it to England; I therefore sent my ser-

servant back with orders to fetch it: but, at his return, he acquainted me that it was not to be found, and that the black-snake was in the same position wherein I had first discovered it. I mention this as an instance of the intrepid nature of the black-snake, which, though not venomous, will attack and devour the rattle-snake, and, in some cases, it is asserted, even dare to assault a man.

May 30. I left Fredericsburg, and having ferried over the Rappahannoc at the fall, travelled that night to Neville's ordinary, about thirty-four miles.

May 31. I passed over the Pignut and Blue Ridges; and, crossing the Shenando, arrived, after a long day's journey of above fifty miles, at Winchester.

The Pignut ridge is a continuation of the south west mountains. It is no where very high; and at the gap where I passed, the ascent is so extremely easy, owing to the winding of the road between the mountains, that I was scarcely sensible of it.

The tract of country lying between this ridge and the coast, is supposed, and with some appearance of probability, to have been gained from the ocean. The situation is extremely low; and the ground every where broken into small hills, nearly of the same elevation, with deep intermediate gullies, as if it were the effect of some sudden retiring of the waters. The soil is principally of sand; and there are few, if any pebbles, within a hundred miles of the shore; for which reason the Virginians in these parts never shoe their horses. Incredible quantities of what are commonly called scallop-shells, are found also near the surface of the ground; and many of the hills are entirely formed of them. These phænomena, with others less obvious to common observation, seem to indicate that the Atlantic, either gradually, or by some sudden revo-
lution

lution in nature, has retired, and loft a confiderable part of that dominion which formerly belonged to it.

The Blue-ridge is much higher than the Pignut: though even thefe mountains are not to be compared with the Alleghenny. To the fouthward, indeed, I was told, they are more lofty; and but little, if at all, inferior to them. The pafs at Afhby's Gap, from the foot of the mountain on the eaftern fide to the Shenando, which runs at the foot on the weftern, is about four miles. The afcent is no where very fteep; though the mountains are, upon the whole, I think, higher than any I have ever feen in England. When I was got to the top, I was inexpreffibly delighted with the fcene which opened before me. Immediately under the mountain, which was covered with chamœdaphnes in full bloom, was a moft beautiful river: beyond this an extenfive plain, diverfified with every pleafing object that nature can exhibit; and, at the diftance of fifty miles, another ridge of ftill more lofty mountains, called the Great, or North-ridge*, which inclofed and terminated the whole.

The river Shenando rifes a great way to the fouthward from under this Great North-ridge. It runs through Augufta County, and falls into the Potowmac fomewhere in Frederic. At the place where I ferried over, it is only about a hundred yards wide; and indeed it is no where, I believe, very broad. It is exceedingly romantic and beautiful, forming great variety of falls, and is fo tranfparent, that you may fee the fmalleft pebble at the depth of eight or ten feet. There is plenty of trout and other fifh in it; but it is not navigable, except for rafts. In fudden frefhes it rifes above forty or fifty feet. The low grounds upon the banks of this river are very rich and fertile; they are chiefly fettled by Germans, who gain a fufficient live-

---

* All thefe ridges confift of fingle mountains joined together, and run parallel to each other.

lihood by raising stock for the troops, and sending butter down into the lower parts of the country. I could not but reflect with pleasure on the situation of these people; and think if there is such a thing as happiness in this life, that they enjoy it. Far from the bustle of the world, they live in the most delightful climate, and richest soil imaginable; they are every where surrounded with beautiful prospects, and sylvan scenes; lofty mountains, transparent streams, falls of water, rich vallies, and majestic woods; the whole intersperfed with an infinite variety of flowering shrubs, constitute the landscape surrounding them: they are subject to few diseases; are generally robust; and live in perfect liberty: they are ignorant of want, and acquainted with but few vices. Their inexperience of the elegancies of life, precludes any regret that they possess not the means of enjoying them: but they possess what many princes would give half their dominions for, health, content, and tranquillity of mind.

Winchester is a small town of about two hundred houses. It is the place of general rendezvous of the Virginian troops, which is the reason of its late rapid increase, and present flourishing condition. The country about it, before the reduction of Fort du Quesne, was greatly exposed to the ravages of the Indians, who daily committed most horrid cruelties: even the town would have been in danger, had not colonel Washington, in order to cover and protect it, erected a fort upon an eminence at one end of it, which proved of the utmost utility; for although the Indians were frequently in sight of the town, they never dared to approach within reach of the fort. It is a regular square fortification, with four bastions, mounting twenty-four cannon; the length of each curtain, if I am not mistaken, is about eighty yards. Within, there are barracks for 450 men. The materials of which it is built, are

F   logs loggs filled up with earth: the soldiers attempted to surround it with a dry ditch; but the rock was so extremely hard and impenetrable, that they were obliged to desist. It is still unfinished; and, I fear, going to ruin; for the assembly, who seldom look a great way before them, after having expended about 9000 l. currency upon it, cannot be prevailed upon to give another thousand towards finishing it, because we are in possession of Pitsburg; and, as they suppose, quite secure on that account: yet it is certain, that, in case of another Indian war on this side, which is by no means improbable, considering our general treatment of that people, it would be of the utmost advantage and security.

There is a peculiarity in the water at Winchester, owing, I was told, to the soil's being of a limy quality, which is frequently productive of severe gripings, especially in strangers; but it is generally supposed, on the other hand, to be a specific against some other diseases.

During my stay at this place, I was almost induced to make a tour for a fortnight to the southward, in Augusta county, for the sake of seeing some natural curiosities; which, the officers assured me, were extremely well worth visiting: but as the Cherokees had been scalping in those parts only a few days before; and as I feared, at the same time, that it would detain me too long, and that I should lose my passage to England, I judged it prudent to decline it.

The curiosities they mentioned to me, were chiefly these:

1. About forty miles westward of Augusta court-house, a beautiful cascade, bursting out of the side of a rock; and, after running some distance through a meadow, rushing down a precipice 150 feet perpendicular.

2. To the southward of this about twenty miles, two curious hot springs, one tasting like alum, the other like the washings of a gun.

3. A most

3. A most extraordinary cave.

4. A medicinal spring, specific in venereal cases. A soldier in the Virginian regiment, whose case was almost desperate, by drinking and bathing in these waters, was, after a few days, intirely cured. This fact was asserted very strongly by some officers, who had been posted there: but colonel Washington, of whom I enquired more particularly concerning it, informed me that he had never heard of it; that he was not indeed at the place where it is said to have happened, but that having the command of the regiment at that time, he should probably have been informed of it. What credit therefore is to be given to it, the reader must judge for himself.

5. Sixty miles southward of Augusta court-house, a natural arch, or bridge, joining two high mountains, with a considerable river running underneath.

6. A river called Lost river, from its sinking under a mountain, and never appearing again.

7. A spring of a sulphureous nature, an infallible cure for particular cutaneous disorders.

8. Sixteen miles north-east of Winchester, a natural cave or well, into which, at times, a person may go down to the depth of 100 or 150 yards; and at other times, the water rises up to the top, and overflows plentifully. This is called the ebbing and flowing well, and is situated in a plain, flat country, not contiguous to any mountain or running water.

9. A few miles from hence, six or seven curious caves communicating with each other.

A day or two before I left Winchester, I discovered that I had been robbed by my servant: he confessed the fact, and pleaded so little in justification of himself, that I was obliged to dismiss him. This distressed me very much, for it was impossible to hire a servant in these parts, or even any one to go over the mountains with me into the lower settlements. However, by the politeness of the commander of the place, the honourable colonel Byrd, and of another gentleman of my acquaintance, I got over these difficulties; for the former, while I continued at Winchester, accommodated me with his own apartments in the fort, ordering his servants to attend and wait upon me; and the latter sent a Negroe boy with me, as far as colonel Washington's, eighty miles distant from this place. On the 4th of June, therefore, I was enabled to leave Winchester, and I travelled that night about eighteen miles, to Sniker's ferry upon the Shenando.

The next morning I repassed the Blue-ridge at Williams's Gap, and proceeded on my journey about forty miles. I this day fell into conversation with a planter, who overtook me on the road, concerning the rattle-snake, of which there are infinite numbers in these parts; and he told me, that one day going to a mill at some distance, he provoked one to such a degree, as to make it strike a small vine which grew close by, and that the vine presently drooped, and died *.

My accommodations this evening were extremely bad; I had been wet to the skin in the afternoon; and at the miserable plantation in which I had taken shelter, I could get no fire; nothing to eat or drink but pure water; and not even a blanket to cover me. I threw myself down upon my mattrass, but suffered so much from cold, and was so infested with insects and vermin, that I could not close my eyes. I rose early in the

* Several persons to whom I have mentioned this fact, have seemed to doubt of the probability of it. But were it not true, a question will naturally arise, how an idea of that nature should occur to an ignorant planter, living remote from all cultivated society; and, more particularly, how he should happen to fix upon that tree; which, supposing the thing possible, is the most likely to have been affected in the manner described.

morn-

morning, therefore, and proceeded upon my journey, being diftant from colonel Wafhington's not more than thirty miles. It was late, however, before I arrived there, for it rained extremely hard, and a man who undertook to fhow me the neareft way, led me among precipices and rocks, and we were loft for above two hours. It was not indeed, without fome compenfation; for he brought me through as beautiful and picturefque a fcene, as eye ever beheld. It was a delightful valley, about two miles in length, and a quarter of one in breadth, between high and craggy mountains, covered with chamœdaphnes or wild ivy, in full flower. Through the middle of the valley glided a rivulet about eight yards wide, extremely lucid, and breaking into innumerable cafcades; and in different parts of it ftood fmall clumps of evergreens; fuch as myrtles, cedars, pines, and various other forts. Upon the whole, not Tempe itfelf could have difplayed greater beauty a more delightful fcene.

At colonel Wafhington's I difpofed of my horfes, and, having borrowed his curricle and fervant, I took leave of Mount-Vernon the 11th of June.

I croffed over the Potowmac into Maryland at Clifton's ferry, where the river is fomething more than a mile broad; and proceeded on my journey to Marlborough, eighteen miles. I here met with a ftrolling company of players, under the direction of one Douglas. I went to fee their theatre, which was a neat, convenient tobacco-houfe, well fitted up for the purpofe. From hence in the afternoon I proceeded to Queen Ann, nine miles; and in the evening nine miles farther, over the Patuxen to London-town ferry; I ftaid here all night, and early in the morning ferrying over South-river, three quarters of a mile in breadth, I arrived at Annapolis, four miles diftant, about nine in the morning.

Anna-

ANNAPOLIS.

Annapolis is the capital of Maryland; it is a small neat town, consisting of about a hundred and fifty houses, situated on a peninsula upon Severn river. The peninsula is formed by the river, and two small creeks; and although the river is not above a mile broad; yet as it falls into Chesapeak bay a little below, there is from this town the finest water-prospect imaginable. The bay is twelve miles over, and beyond it you may discern the eastern shore; so that the scene is diversified with fields, wood, and water. The tide rises here about two feet, and the water is salt, though the distance of the Capes is more than 200 miles. The town is not laid out regularly, but is tolerably well built, and has several good brick houses in it. None of the streets are paved, and the few public buildings here are not worth mentioning. The church is a very poor one, the stadt-house but indifferent, and the governor's palace is not finished. This last mentioned building was begun a few years ago; it is situated very finely upon an eminence, and commands a beautiful view of the town and environs. It has four large rooms on the lower floor, besides a magnificent hall, a stair-case, and a vestibule. On each side of the entrance are four windows, and nine upon the first story; the offices are under ground. It was to have had a fine portico the whole range of the building; but unluckily the governor and assembly disagreeing about ways and means, the execution of the design was suspended; and only the shell of the house has been finished, which is now going to ruin. The house, which the present governor inhabits, is hired by the province at 80 l. currency per annum.

There is very little trade carried on from this place, and the chief of the inhabitants are storekeepers or public officers. They build two or three ships annually, but seldom more.
There

MARYLAND.

There are no fortifications, except a miserable battery of fifteen six-pounders.

Maryland is situated between the 38th and 40th degrees of north latitude, and 75th and 80th of west longitude from London. It is bounded on the east by the Atlantic ocean, and the three lower counties of Delaware; on the south and west by Virginia; and by Pennsylvania on the north. The climate, soil, and natural productions of it are nearly the same as those of Virginia. It is watered by many fine rivers, and almost innumerable creeks; but is far from being well cultivated, and is capable of much improvement. It is divided into fourteen counties, and between forty and fifty parishes; and there are several little towns in it which are neatly built. The inhabitants, exclusive of slaves, are supposed to be about ninety thousand: of which the militia, including all white males between sixteen and sixty, amounts to eighteen. The slaves are about thirty-two thousand. The staple of the country is tobacco; and, communibus annis, they export near 30,000 hogsheads: last year their exports amounted to 50,000. Their manufactures are very trifling. The government is a proprietary one; and consists of the proprietor (viz. lord Baltimore); his governor; the council, composed of twelve persons nominated by himself; and a house of representatives, elected by the people; four for each county, and two for Annapolis. The power of the proprietor is next to regal; of the other parts of the legislature, much the same as in Virginia. The lower house has been at variance some years with the council and governor, concerning ways and means; chiefly in regard to taxing the merchants book-debts: which has been the reason of its having done nothing for the defence of the colonies during the war. The house has constantly voted troops, but as constantly laid the same tax for the maintenance of them: so the

ANNAPOLIS.

council has always rejected it; alledging the inconvenience of such a tax, as it would necessarily be a restraint upon trade; and ruin many of the merchants credit. The proprietor has a negative * upon every bill, exclusive of his governor.

There are several courts of judicature in this province; but the principal are either those which are held quarterly in each county by the justices thereof, like those in Virginia; or the provincial ones, which are held twice annually at Annapolis by judges appointed for that purpose †. The court of chancery consists of the governor and council: and the dernier resort is to his majesty in council at home.

The established religion is that of the church of England: but there are as many Roman Catholics as Protestants. The clergy are liberally provided for; they have not, as in Virginia, a fixed quantity of tobacco; but so much per head, viz. 30 weight for every tythable in their respective parishes: and some of them make more than 300 l. sterling per annum. They are presented to their livings by the governor; and are under the jurisdiction of the bishop of London; but being at a great distance from England, and having no commissary to superintend their affairs, they labour under many inconveniences. Assessments are made, I was told, by the county-courts; the vestry, which consists of twelve members distinct from the church-wardens, having little or no authority ‡.

* This power is doubted, though it has never yet been contested.

† Besides these courts, there was formerly a general court of assize held throughout the province, either once or twice a year, but this has been laid aside.

‡ The whole vestry, as in Virginia, consists of twelve members; but they go off by rotation two every year; so there is annually a fresh election. They have the power of appointing inspectors, &c.

In

In each county throughout this province, there is a public free-school, for reading, writing, and accounts; but no college or academy; and the education of youth is but little attended to.

The character of the inhabitants is much the same as that of the Virginians; and the state of the two colonies nearly alike. Tobacco, to speak in general, is the chief thing attended to in both. There have been some attempts indeed to make wine; and it is certain, that the country is capable of producing almost any sort of grapes. Col. Tasco, a gentleman of distinction in these parts, attempted to make Burgundy, and succeeded tolerably well, for the first trial. I drank some of the wine at the table of Mr. Hamilton, the governor of Pensylvania, and thought it not bad. But whether, as this gentleman is now dead, any other person will have spirit to prosecute his plan, I much doubt. The currency here is paper-money, and the difference of exchange about fifty per cent. The duty upon negroes, is only forty shillings currency per head at their importation; whereas in Virginia it is ten pounds.

I hired a schooner of about ten ton, and embarked for the head of the bay, distant twenty-three leagues; we made sail with a fresh breeze, and after a pleasant passage of sixteen hours, in one of the most delightful days imaginable, arrived at Frederick-Town upon Sassafras river, about twelve in the evening. I never in my life spent a day more agreeable, or with higher entertainment. The shores on each side the bay, and the many little islands interspersed in it, afford very beautiful prospects; we were entertained at the same time with innumerable porpoises playing about the bow of the ship; and naturally fell into a train of the most pleasing reflections, on observing the mouths of the many noble rivers as we passed along. On the western shore, besides those great rivers of Virginia, which I have already described, there are ten or eleven others large and capacious, some of them navigable a considerable

1760.

June 13.

G way

way up into the country. "The Patuxen, which we have left behind us, said the master of the schooner as we were sailing over this beautiful bay, is navigable near fifty miles for vessels of three hundred ton burthen. Yonder, he added, are South and Severn rivers, navigable above ten miles. A little farther is the Patapsico, a large and noble river; where I have gone up fifteen miles. Gunpowder and Bush rivers admit only sloops and schooners. The Susquehannah, though so majestic, and superior in appearance, has only a short, and that a bad navigation; but it rises an immense way off in unknown and inhospitable regions, is exceedingly large and beautiful, and affords great variety of fish. On the eastern shore, he concluded, are Bahama, Sassafras, Chester, Wye, Miles, Great Choptank, Little Choptank, Nanticote, Manokin, and Pocomoke rivers; all of them navigable, more or less, for several miles."—Such was our conversation and entertainment during this delightful voyage.

Frederic-town is a small village on the western side of Sassafras river, built for the accommodation of strangers and travellers; on the eastern side, exactly opposite to it, is another small village (George-town), erected for the same purpose. Having hired an Italian chaise, with a servant and horse to attend me as far as Philadelphia, I left Frederic-town the next day, and went to Newcastle, thirty-two miles.

Newcastle is situated upon Delaware river, about forty miles above the Bay, and a hundred from the Capes. It is the capital of the three lower counties, but a place of very little consideration; there are scarcely more than an hundred houses in it, and no public buildings that deserve to be taken notice of. The church, presbyterian and quakers meeting-houses, court-house, and market-house, are almost equally bad, and undeserving of attention.

The province, of which this is the capital, and which is distinguished by the name of the Three Lower Counties of Newcastle,

castle, Suffex, and Kent, belonged formerly to the Dutch; but was ratified to the crown of England, by the treaty of Breda; it was afterward fold by the duke of York to the proprietor of Penfylvania, and has continued a feparate government, though nearly under the fame regulations with that province, ever fince. The fame governor prefides over both; but the affembly, and courts of judicature are different: different as to their conftituent members, for in form they are nearly alike. The affembly confifts of eighteen perfons, elected annually by the people; fix for each county: this with the governor, forms the legiflature of the province. There is a militia, in which all perfons, from eighteen to fifty, are obliged to be inrolled; and the county of Newcaftle alone furnifhes more than feven hundred.

The next day I fet out for Philadelphia, diftant about thirty-fix miles, and arrived there in the evening. The country all the way bore a different afpect from any thing I had hitherto feen in America. It was much better cultivated, and beautifully laid out into fields of clover, grain, and flax. I paffed by a very pretty village called Wilmington; and rode through two others, viz. Chefter and Derby. The Delaware river is in fight great part of the way, and is three miles broad. Upon the whole nothing could be more pleafing than the ride which I had this day. I ferried over the Schuilkill, about three miles below Philadelphia; from whence to the city the whole country is covered with villas, gardens, and luxuriant orchards.

Philadelphia, if we confider that not eighty years ago the place where it now ftands was a wild and uncultivated defart, inhabited by nothing but ravenous beafts, and a favage people, muft certainly be the object of every one's wonder and admiration. It is fituated upon a tongue of land, a few miles above the confluence of the Delaware and Schuilkill; and contains about 3000 houfes, and 18 or 20,000 inhabitants. It is built north and south upon the banks of the Delaware; and is nearly two miles in length, and three quarters of one in breadth. The streets are laid out with great regularity in parallel lines, intersected by others at right angles, and are handsomely built: on each side there is a pavement of broad stones for foot passengers; and in most of them a causeway in the middle for carriages. Upon dark nights it is well lighted, and watched by a patrole: there are many fair houses, and public edifices in it. The stadt-house is a large, handsome, though heavy building; in this are held the councils, the assemblies, and supreme courts; there are apartments in it also for the accommodation of Indian chiefs or sachems; likewise two libraries; one belonging to the province, the other to a society, which was incorporated about ten years ago, and consists of sixty members. Each member upon admission, subscribed forty shillings; and afterward annually ten. They can alienate their shares, by will or deed, to any person approved of by the society. They have a small collection of medals and medallions, and a few other curiosities, such as the skin of a rattle-snake killed at Surinam twelve feet long; and several Northern Indian habits made of furs and skins. At a small distance from the stadt-house, there is is another fine library, consisting of a very valuable and chosen collection of books, left by a Mr. Logan; they are chiefly in the learned languages. Near this there is also a noble hospital for lunatics, and other sick persons. Besides these buildings, there are spacious barracks for 17 or 1800 men; a good assembly-room belonging to the society of free-masons; and eight or ten places of religious worship; viz. two churches, three quakers meeting-houses, two presbyterian ditto, one Lutheran church, one Dutch Calvinist ditto, one Swedish ditto, one Romish chapel, one anabaptist meeting-house, one Moravian ditto: there is also an academy or college, originally built for a tabernacle for Mr. Whitefield.

At

At the fouth-end of the town, upon the river, there is a battery mounting thirty guns, but it is in a ftate of decay. It was defigned as a check upon privateers. Thefe, with a few almshoufes, and a fchool-houfe belonging to the quakers, are the chief public buildings in Philadelphia. The city is in a very flourifhing ftate, and inhabited by merchants, artifts, tradefmen, and perfons of all occupations. There is a public market held twice a week, upon Wednefday and Saturday, almoft equal to that of Leadenhall, and a tolerable one every day befides. The ftreets are crowded with people, and the river with veffels. Houfes are fo dear, that they will let for 100 l. currency per annum; and lots, not above thirty feet in breadth, and a hundred in length, in advantageous fituations, will fell for 1000 l. fterling. There are feveral docks upon the river, and about twenty-five veffels are built there annually. I counted upon the ftocks at one time no lefs than feventeen, moft of them three-mafted veffels.

Can the mind have a greater pleafure than in contemplating the rife and progrefs of cities and empires? Than in perceiving a rich and opulent ftate arifing out of a fmall fettlement or colony? This pleafure every one muft feel who confiders Penfylvania. —This wonderful province is fituated between the 40th and 43d degrees of north latitude, and about 76 degrees weft longitude from London, in a healthy and delightful climate, amidft all the advantages that nature can beftow. The foil is extremely ftrong and fertile, and produces fpontaneoufly an infinite variety of trees, flowers, fruits, and plants of different forts. The mountains are enriched with ore, and the rivers with fifh: fome of thefe are fo ftately as not to be beheld without admiration: the Delaware is navigable for large veffels as far as the falls, 180 miles diftant from the fea, and 120 from the bay. At the mouth it is more than three miles broad, and above one at Philadelphia. The navigation is obftructed

PENSYLVANIA.

ſtructed in the winter, for about ſix weeks, by the ſeverity of the froſt; but, at other times, it is bold and open. The Schuilkill, though not navigable for any great ſpace, is exceedingly romantic, and affords the moſt delightful retirements.

Cultivation is carried to a high degree of perfection; and Penſylvania produces not only great plenty, but alſo great variety of grain; it yields likewiſe flax-ſeed, hemp, cattle of different kinds, and various other articles *.

It is divided into eight counties, and contains many large and populous towns: Carliſle, Lancaſter, and German-town, conſiſt each of near five hundred houſes; there are ſeveral others which have from one to two hundred.

The number of inhabitants is ſuppoſed to be between four and five hundred thouſand, a fifth of which are quakers; there are very few Negroes or ſlaves.

The trade of Penſylvania is ſurpriſingly extenſive, carried on to Great Britain, the Weſt Indies, every part of North America, the Madeiras, Liſbon, Cadiz, Holland, Africa, the Spaniſh main, and ſeveral other places; excluſive of what is illicitly carried on to Cape François, and Monte-Chriſto. Their exports are proviſions of all kinds, lumber, hemp, flax, flax-ſeed, iron, furrs, and deer-ſkins. Their imports, Engliſh ma-

* In the ſouthern colonies cultivation is in a very low ſtate. The common proceſs of it is, firſt to cut off the trees two or three feet above ground, in order to let in the ſun and air, leaving the ſtumps to decay and rot, which they do in a few years. After this they dig and plant, and continue to work the ſame fields, year after year, without ever manuring it, till it is quite ſpent. They then enter upon a freſh piece of ground, allowing this a reſpite of about twenty years to recover itſelf; during which time it becomes beautifully covered with Virginian pines: the ſeeds of that tree, which are exceedingly ſmall, and, when the cones open, are wafted through the air in great abundance, ſowing themſelves in every vacant ſpot of neglected ground.

nufactures,

nufactures, with the superfluities and luxuries of life. By their flag of truce-trade, they also get sugar, which they refine and send to Europe.

Their manufactures are very considerable. The Germantown thread-stockings are in high estimation; and the year before last, I have been credibly informed, there were manufactured in that town alone, above 60,000 dozen pair. Their common retail price is a dollar per pair.

The Irish settlers make very good linens: some woollens have also been fabricated, but not I believe to any amount. There are several other manufactures, viz. of beaver hats, which are superior in goodness to any in Europe, of cordage, linseed-oil, starch, myrtle-wax and spermaceti candles, soap, earthen ware, and other commodities.

The government of this province is a proprietary one. The legislature is lodged in the hands of a governor, appointed (with the king's approbation) by the proprietor; and a house of representatives, elected by the people, consisting of thirty-seven members. These are of various religious persuasions; for by the charter of privileges, which Mr. Penn granted to the settlers in Pensylvania, no person who believed in God could be molested in his calling or profession; and any one who believed in Jesus Christ might enjoy the first post under the government. The crown has reserved to itself a power of repealing any law, which may interfere with the prerogative, or be contrary to the laws of Great Britain.

The judicature consists of different courts. The justices of the peace, who, together with the other judges, are of the governor's appointment, hold quarterly sessions conformable to the laws of England; and, when these are finished, continue to sit in quality of judges of common pleas, by a special commission. The supreme court consists of a chief justice, and

two

two affiftant judges; they have the united authority of the King's Bench, Common Pleas, and Court of Exchequer. They not only receive appeals, but all caufes once commenced in the inferior courts, after the firft writ, may be moved thither by a habeas corpus, certiorari, writ of error, &c. The judges of the fupreme court have alfo a ftanding and diftinct commiffion, to hold, as fhall feem needful, courts of oyer and terminer, and general goal-deliveries throughout the province; but this power they feldom, I believe, exercife. The fupreme courts are held twice a year at Philadelphia. There is no Court of Chancery; but the want of it is fupplied, in fome meafure, by the other courts. There is a particular officer called the regifter-general, appointed by the governor, whofe authority extends over the whole province, where he has feveral deputies. He grants letters of adminiftration, and probates of wills. In cafes of difpute, or caveat entered, he may call in, as affiftants, two juftices of the peace. The governor can pardon in all cafes, except of treafon or murder, and then can reprieve till he knows the king's pleafure.

There is here, as in moft of the other colonies, a Court of Vice-admiralty, held by commiffion from the Admiralty in England, for the trial of captures and of piracies, and other mifdemeanors committed upon the high feas; but there lies an appeal from it, I believe, to the Court of Delegates in England.

As to religion, there is none properly eftablifhed; but Proteftants of all denominations, Papifts, Jews, and all other fects whatfoever, are univerfally tolerated. There are twelve clergymen of the church of England, who are fent by the Society for the Propagation of the Gofpel, and are allowed annually 50l. each, befides what they get from fubfcriptions and furplice fees. Some few of thefe are itinerant miffionaries, and have no fixed refidence, but travel from place to place, as occafion casion requires, upon the frontiers. They are under the jurisdiction of the bishop of London.

Arts and sciences are yet in their infancy. There are some few persons who have discovered a taste for music and painting; and philosophy seems not only to have made a considerable progress already, but to be daily gaining ground. The library society is an excellent institution for propagating a taste for literature; and the college well calculated to form and cultivate it. This last institution is erected upon an admirable plan, and is by far the best school for learning throughout America. It has been chiefly raised by contributions; and its present fund is about 10,000 l. Pensylvania money. An account of it may be seen in Dr. Smith's (the president's) Discourses. The quakers also have an academy for instructing their youth in classical learning, and practical mathematics: there are three teachers, and about seventy boys in it. Besides these, there are several schools in the province for the Dutch and other foreign children; and a considerable one is going to be erected at German-town.

The Pensylvanians, as to character, are a frugal and industrious people: not remarkably courteous and hospitable to strangers, unless particularly recommended to them; but rather, like the denizens of most commercial cities, the reverse. They are great republicans, and have fallen into the same errors in their ideas of independency, as most of the other colonies have. They are by far the most enterprizing people upon the continent. As they consist of several nations, and talk several languages, they are aliens in some respect to Great Britain: nor can it be expected that they should have the same filial attachment to her which her own immediate offspring have. However, they are quiet, and concern themselves but little, except about getting money. The women are

are exceedingly handsome and polite; they are naturally sprightly and fond of pleasure; and, upon the whole, are much more agreeable and accomplished than the men. Since their intercourse with the English officers, they are greatly improved; and, without flattery, many of them would not make bad figures even in the first assemblies in Europe. Their amusements are chiefly dancing, in the winter; and, in the summer, forming parties of pleasure upon the Schuilkill, and in the country. There is a society of sixteen ladies, and as many gentlemen, called the fishing company, which meet once a fortnight upon the Schuilkill. They have a very pleasant room erected in a romantic situation upon the banks of that river, where they generally dine and drink tea. There are several pretty walks about it, and some wild and rugged rocks, which, together with the water and fine groves that adorn the banks, form a most beautiful and picturesque scene. There are boats and fishing tackle of all sorts, and the company divert themselves with walking, fishing, going upon the water, dancing, singing, conversing, or just as they please. The ladies wear an uniform, and appear with great ease and advantage from the neatness and simplicity of it. The first and most distinguished people of the colony are of this society; and it is very advantageous to a stranger to be introduced to it, as he hereby gets acquainted with the best and most respectable company in Philadelphia. In the winter, when there is snow upon the ground, it is usual to make what they call sleighing parties, or to go upon it in sledges; but as this is a practice well known in Europe, it is needless to describe it.

The present state of Pensylvania is undoubtedly very flourishing. The country is well cultiuated, and there are not less than 9000 waggons employed in it, in different services. Till this war they were exempt from taxes; and it was not without

out difficulty that the quakers were prevailed upon to grant any supplies for the defence of the frontiers, though exposed to the most horrid cruelties: it was not from principle, say their enemies, that they refused it, but from interest; for as they were the first settlers, they chiefly occupy the interior and lower parts of the province, and are not exposed to incursions. At length, however, compelled by clamour and public discontent, they were obliged to pass a supply bill for 100,000 l. to raise five and twenty hundred men, and these they have kept up ever since; they afterwards passed a militia bill, but it was such an one as answered no good purpose. The quakers have much the greatest influence in the assembly, and are supported there by the Dutch and Germans, who are as averse to taxes as themselves. Their power, however, at present seems rather on the decline, which is the reason, as the opposite party pretend, that they stir up on all occasions as much confusion as possible, from that trite maxim in politics, divide et impera. They have quarrelled with the proprietors upon several occasions, whether altogether justly or not, I will not pretend to say; it is certain, however, that the determinations at home have been sometimes in their favour. The late subjects of their disputes have been chiefly these:

First, Whether the proprietary lands ought to be taxed? This has been determined at home in the affirmative.

Secondly, Whether the proprietor ought to have any choice or approbation of the assessors?

Thirdly, Whether he ought to give his governor instructions? And,

Lastly, Whether the judges of his appointment ought to be during pleasure, or quamdiu se bene gesserint? These three last are still undecided.

Upon the whole, though this province is exceedingly flourishing, yet there are certainly great abuses in it; and such as, if not speedily rectified, will be productive of bad consequences.

The difference of exchange between bills and the currency of Pensylvania, is about 75 per cent.

An occurrence happened to me at Philadelphia, which though in itself of a trifling nature, I cannot but take notice of, as a singular instance of the strong possession which an idea will sometimes take of the mind; so as totally to derange it. A lady from Rhode-Island, who lodged in the same house with myself, had an unfortunate brother in the infirmary, a lunatic. He was supposed to be nearly well, and was permitted occasionally to see company. A few days before I was to leave Philadelphia, this lady invited me to accompany her in one of her visits to him, adding, that on her inadvertently mentioning to him some circumstances relating to me, he had expressed a most earnest desire to see me. I strongly objected to the proposal, urging the impropriety of introducing a stranger, or, indeed, company of any sort, to a person in that unhappy situation; as it might possibly agitate his mind, and retard his recovery. I advised her therefore not to take any further notice of it; hoping he might forget, or not mention it any more. The next day she renewed her application, adding, that her brother was exceedingly disappointed; and intreated me to attend her in so pressing a manner, that I could not with civility refuse it. On entering the cell, a beam of satisfaction seemed to dart from his eye, not easy to be expressed or conceived. I took him by the hand; and, seating myself opposite the bed to which he was chained, immediately took the lead in conversation, talking of indifferent matters, such as I thought, could not possibly

bly

bly tend to interest or disturb his mind. I had not proceeded far when he suddenly interrupted me; and proposed a question, which at once convinced me that he was in a very unfit state to see company. I immediately therefore rose up; and making an excuse that my engagements that day would not admit of my entering into so curious a subject, desired him to reserve it for some future conversation. He seemed greatly disconcerted; but being near the door which stood open, I took my leave and retired. The next morning I left Philadelphia; nor did I think any more of this occurrence till I arrived at Rhode-Island; where I was informed, that the chief, if not sole, instances of insanity shewn by this unhappy young man, were some attempts which he had made to kill a clergyman of the church of England. That he had been educated to be a teacher amongst the congregationalists, but had taken it into his head, that he could never gain heaven, or be happy, but by committing so heroic and meritorious an action. The very evening of his confinement he was prevented from fulfilling his purpose, in the instant that he was raising up his hand to plunge a knife into the back of a clergyman, who was reading the funeral service, in the presence of a large congregation. What his intentions were in regard to myself, I cannot pretend to say; he offered me no violence: but those at Rhode-Island of his acquaintance, to whom I related this transaction, were fully persuaded that he was far from being cured of his distemper *.

* Since my return to Europe, I have been informed of an instance similar to this, which happened at Florence. A gentleman had taken it into his head that a very large diamond lay buried under a mountain which stood upon his estate, and was near ruining himself and his family by digging for it. His friends, by some contrivance or other, got him away to Florence, and placed him under the care of the late celebrated Dr. Cocchi. He there appeared per-

I left

PENSYLVANIA. THE JERSEYS.

I left Philadelphia the 6th of July, and travelled in the ſtage as far as Sheminey-ferry, about ſeventeen miles; where I was overtaken by a gentleman and ſome ladies of my acquaintance, who were going a few miles farther upon a party of pleaſure. They were ſo obliging as to make room for me in one of their chaiſes, and we proceeded and dined together at Briſtol, a ſmall town upon the Delaware, oppoſite Burlington: in the afternoon we went ten miles higher up the river, and ferried over to Trenton, ſituated in the Jerſeys. This is built on the eaſt ſide of the Delaware, and contains about a hundred houſes. It has nothing remarkable; there is a church, a quakers and preſbyterian meeting-houſe, and barracks for three hundred men. From hence we went to Sir John Sinclair's, at the Falls of Delaware, about a mile above Trenton, a pleaſant rural retirement; where we ſpent a moſt agreeable evening. In the morn-

feƈtly compoſed, talked very rationally, and, having been well educated, afforded great entertainment to the doƈtor and his friends, who converſed with him. One day as they were ſitting together, he mentiond to the doƈtor, that it was very hard he ſhould be deprived of his liberty, when he was perfeƈtly well; and that it was only a ſcheme of his relations to keep him in confinement, in order that they might enjoy his eſtate. The doƈtor, who had perceived no marks of inſanity, began to be ſtaggered; and promiſed, in caſe he ſhould ſee no reaſon to alter his ſentiments, to ſign a certificate of his being well on ſuch a day, in order to its being ſent to England, that he might have his releaſe. The day arrived, and the doƈtor was preparing to perform his promiſe; but, whether by deſign on perceiving ſomething particular in the looks of his patient, or by accident, I could not learnt, he ſaid to the gentleman; "Now, Sir, I beg from this time that you will think no more of this " fooliſh affair of the mountain and diamond." "Not think of the diamond, ſaid the madman; " it is for this reaſon that I want my liberty; I know ex- " aƈtly the ſpot where it lies; and I will have it in my poſſeſſion, before I am " a year older."

This ſtory was related to me in Tuſcany, and I had no reaſon to queſtion the truth of it.

ing, the company returned to Philadelphia; and, having hired a chaise, I proceeded to Prince-town, twelve miles distant.

At this place, there is a handsome school and college for the education of Dissenters; erected upon the plan of those in Scotland. There are about twenty boys in the grammar-school, and sixty in the college: at present there are only two professors, besides the provost; but they intend, as their fund increases, which is yet very small, and does not exceed 2000 l. currency, to add to this number. The building is extremely convenient, airy, and spacious; and has a chapel and other proper offices. Two students are in each set of apartments, which consists of a large bed-room, with a fire-place, and two studies. There is a small collection of books, a few instruments, and some natural curiosities. The expence to a student for room-rent, commons, and tutorage, amounts to about 25 l. currency per year. The provost has a salary of 200 l. currency, and the professors 50 l. each. The name of the college is Nassau-Hall.—From hence, in the afternoon, I proceeded to Brunswick, eighteen miles farther, a small city of about a hundred houses, situated upon Raritan river; where there are also very neat barracks for 300 men, a church, and a presbyterian meeting-house. It is celebrated for the number of its beauties; and, indeed, at this place and Philadelphia, were the handsomest women that I saw in America. At a small distance from the town is a copper-mine belonging to a Mr. French, (I was told) a pretty good one. The next day I rode up the river, about nine miles to the Raritan hills, to see a small cascade, which falls about fifteen or twenty feet, very romanticly, from between two rocks. The country I passed through is exceedingly rich and beautiful; and the banks of the river are covered with gentlemen's houses. At one of these I had an opportu‑

nity

nity of feeing fome good portraits of Vandyke, and feveral other fmall Dutch paintings.

On Monday the 7th, I proceeded to Perth-Amboy, twelve miles, the capital of the Eaft-Jerfeys, which is pleafantly fituated upon a neck of land, included between the Raritan and Amboy rivers and a large open bay. This is generally the place of the governor's refidence; and alternately, here and at Burlington, the capital of the Weft Jerfeys, are held the affemblies, and other public meetings; it contains about a hundred houfes, and has very fine bartacks for 300 men. In the afternoon I travelled fixteen miles farther to Elizabeth-town, leaving Woodbridge, a fmall village where there is a printing-office, a little on my right hand. Elizabeth-town, is built upon a fmall creek or river that falls into Newark-bay, and contains between two and three hundred houfes. It has a court-houfe, a church, and a meeting-houfe; and barracks alfo like thofe abovementioned.

The next morning I rode out, in order to vifit Pafaic Falls, diftant about twenty-three miles, and had a very agreeable tour. After riding about fix miles, I came to a town called Newark, built in an irregular fcattered manner, after the fafhion of fome of our villages in England, near two miles in length. It has a church erected in the Gothic tafte with a fpire, the firft I had feen in America; and fome other inconfiderable public buildings. Immediately on my leaving this place, I came upon the banks of Second, or Pafaic river, along which I travelled about eighteen miles to the Falls, through a rich country, covered with fine fields and gentlemen's feats.

The Falls are very extraordinary, different from any thing I had hitherto met with in America. The river is about forty yards broad, and runs with a very fwift current, till coming to a deep chafm or cleft which croffes the channel, it falls above

feventy

seventy feet perpendicular in one intire sheet. One end of the
cleft is closed up, and the water rushes out at the other with
incredible rapidity, in an acute angle to its former direction;
and is received into a large bason. From hence it takes a
winding course through the rocks, and spreads again into a very
considerable channel. The cleft is from four to twelve feet
broad. The spray formed two beautiful (viz. the primary and
secondary) rainbows, and helped to make as fine a scene as ima-
gination could conceive. This extraordinary phenomenon is
supposed to have been produced by an earthquake. The fate of
two Indians is delivered down by tradition, who, venturing too
near the Falls in a canoe, were carried down the precipice, and
dashed to pieces. About thirty yards above the great Fall, is
another, a most beautiful one, gliding over some ledges of rocks
each two or three feet perpendicular, which heightens the scene
very much.

From hence I returned, and in my way crossed over the river to colonel John Schuyler's copper mines, where there is a
very rich vein of ore, and a fire-engine erected upon common
principles.

After this I went down two miles farther to the park and
gardens of this gentleman's brother, colonel Peter Schuyler. In
the gardens is a very large collection of citrons, oranges, limes,
lemons, balsams of Peru, aloes, pomegranates, and other tro-
pical plants; and in the park I saw several American and English deer, and three or four elks or moose-deer. I arrived at
Elizabeth town in the evening, not a little entertained with my
expedition, but exceedingly fatigued with the violent heat of
the weather, and the many mosquitoes that had infested me.

Before I take leave of the Jerseys, it is necessary I should
give some account of this province. New Jersey is situated between the 39th and 42d degrees of north latitude, and about

NEW JERSEY.

seventy-five degrees west longitude: it is bounded on the east by the Atlantic, on the west by Pensylvania, or to speak more properly the Delaware; on the south by Delaware-bay; and on the north by Hudson's river and the province of New York. The climate is nearly the same as that of Pensylvania: and the soil, which is a kind of red slate, is so exceedingly rich, that in a short time after it has been turned up and exposed to the air and moisture, it is converted into a species of marle *.

New Jersey has very great natural advantages of hills, valleys, rivers, and large bays. The Delaware is on one side, and Hudson's river on the other; besides which it has the Raritan, Pasaic, and Amboy rivers; and Newark, and New York bays. It produces vast quantities of grain, besides hemp, flax, hay, Indian corn, and other articles. It is divided into eleven counties, and has several small towns, though not one of consideration. The number of its inhabitants is supposed to be 70,000: of which, all males, between sixteen and sixty, Negroes excepted, are obliged to serve in the militia. There is no foreign trade carried on from this province; for the inhabitants sell their produce to the merchants of Philadelphia and New York, and take in return European goods and other necessaries of life. They have some trifling manufactures of their own, but nothing that deserves mentioning.

The government consists of a governor, twelve counsellors, and a house of representatives of about twenty-six members,

---

* Since my return from America, I have met with a gentleman (Edward Wortley Montagu, esq.) who had visited the Holy Land. He described the soil of that country to be similar in almost every circumstance to this of the Jerseys. He said, it appeared to be of a red slaty substance, sterile, and incapable of producing any thing worth the cultivation; but that being broken up and exposed to the air, it became exceedingly mellow, and was fertile in the highest degree.

the two former nominated by the king, the latter elected by the people. Each branch has a negative; they meet at Amboy and at Burlington alternately. The governor's falary, with perquifites, is about 800, or 1000 l. fterling a year; he is not allowed a houfe to refide in, but is obliged to hire one at his own expence. There are feveral courts of judicature here, much like thofe of the other provinces. The juftices hold quarterly feffions for petty larcenies, and other trifling caufes: and the fupreme judge, with two affiftant juftices, holds, once a year, a general affize, throughout the province, of oyer and terminer, and common-pleas. He holds alfo annually four fupreme courts, alternately at Amboy and Burlington, of king's-bench, common-pleas, and exchequer. The offices of chancellor and vice-admiral, are executed by the governor, and the dernier refort is to his majefty in council.

There is properly no eftablifhed religion in this province, and the inhabitants are of various perfuafions: the fociety fends fix miffionaries, who are generally well received; and the church gains ground daily. Their falaries are about the fame as in Penfylvania.

Arts and fciences are here, as in the other parts of America, juft dawning. The college will in time, without doubt, be of confiderable advantage, but being yet in its infancy, it has not had an opportunity of operating, or effecting any vifible improvement.

The New Jerfey men, as to character, are like moft country gentlemen; good-natured, hofpitable, and of a more liberal turn than their neighbours the Penfylvanians. They live altogether upon their eftates, and are literally gentlemen farmers. The country in its prefent ftate can fcarcely be called flourifhing; for although it is extremely well cultivated, thickly feated, and the garden of North America, yet, having no foreign trade, it is kept under; and deprived of thofe riches and advantages, which it would otherwife foon acquire. There have been fome attempts to remedy this defect, but whether from the difficulty of diverting a thing out of a channel in which it has long flowed; or from want of propriety or perfeverance, in the meafures, I am unable to fay; but the truth is, they have not fucceeded. Upon the whole, however, this province may be called a rich one: during the prefent war it has raifed confiderable fupplies, having feldom had lefs than 1000 men in pay, with a leader (colonel Schuyler) at their head, who has done honour to his country by his patriotic and public fpirit. The paper currency of this colony is at about 70 per cent. difcount, but in very good repute; and preferred by the Penfylvanians and New-Yorkers, even to that of their own provinces.

On Wednefday the 9th of July, I croffed over to Staten Ifland, in the province of New York; and travelled upon it about nine miles to the point which is oppofite New York city.

In my way I had an opportunity of feeing the method of making wampum. This, I am perfuaded the reader knows is the current money amongft the Indians. It is made of the clamfhell; a fhell, confifting within of two colours, purple and white; and in form not unlike a thick oyfter-fhell. The procefs of manufacturing it is very fimple. It is firft clipped to a proper fize, which is that of a fmall oblong parallelopiped, then drilled, and afterward ground to a round fmooth furface, and polifhed. The purple wampum is much more valuable than the white; a very fmall part of the fhell being of that colour.

At the point I embarked for New York; and, after a pleafant paffage over the bay, which is three leagues wide, and va-

rious

rious delightful profpects of rivers, iflands, fields, hills, woods, the Narrows, New-York city, veffels failing to and fro, and innumerable porpoifes playing upon the furface of the water, in an evening fo ferene that the hemifphere was not ruffled by a fingle cloud, arrived there about the fetting of the fun.

This city is fituated upon the point of a fmall ifland, lying open to the bay on one fide, and on the others included between the North and Eaft rivers, and commands a fine profpect of water, the Jerfeys, Long Ifland, Staten Ifland, and feveral others, which lie fcattered in the bay. It contains between 2 and 3000 houfes, and 16 or 17,000 inhabitants, is tolerably well built, and has feveral good houfes. The ftreets are paved, and very clean, but in general they are narrow; there are two or three, indeed, which are fpacious and airy, particularly the Broad Way. The houfes in this ftreet have moft of them a row of trees before them; which form an agreeable fhade, and produce a pretty effect. The whole length of the town is fomething more than a mile; the breadth of it about half an one. The fituation is, I believe, efteemed healthy; but it is fubject to one great inconvenience, which is the want of frefh water; fo that the inhabitants are obliged to have it brought from fprings at fome diftance out of town. There are feveral public buildings, though but few that deferve attention. The college, when finifhed, will be exceedingly handfome: it is to be built on three fides of a quadrangle, fronting Hudfon's or North river, and will be the moft beautifully fituated of any college, I believe, in the world. At prefent only one wing is finifhed, which is of ftone, and confifts of twenty-four fets of apartments; each having a large fitting room, with a ftudy, and bed chamber. They are obliged to make ufe of fome of thefe apartments for a mafter's lodge,

lodge, library, chapel, hall, &c. but as soon as the whole shall be completed, there will be proper apartments for each of these offices. The name of it is King's College.

There are two churches in New York, the old, or Trinity Church, and the new one, or St. George's Chapel; both of them large buildings, the former in the Gothic taste, with a spire, the other upon the model of some of the new churches in London. Besides these, there are several other places of religious worship; namely, two Low Dutch Calvinist churches, one High Dutch ditto, one French ditto, one German Lutheran church, one presbyterian meeting-house, one quakers ditto, one anabaptists do, one Moravian ditto, and a Jews synagogue. There is also a very handsome charity-school for sixty poor boys and girls, a good work-house, barracks for a regiment of soldiers, and one of the finest prisons I have ever seen. The court or stadt-house makes no great figure, but it is to be repaired and beautified. There is a quadrangular fort, capable of mounting sixty cannon, though at present there are, I believe, only thirty-two. Within this is the governor's palace, and underneath it a battery capable of mounting ninety-four guns, and barracks for a company or two of soldiers. Upon one of the islands in the bay is an hospital for sick and wounded seamen; and, upon another, a pest-house. These are the most noted public buildings in and about the city.

The province of New York is situated between the 40th and 45th degrees of north latitude, and about 75 degrees west longitude. It lies in a fine climate, and enjoys a very wholesome air. The soil of most parts of it is extremely good, particularly of Long Island: and it has the advantages of a fine harbour, and fine rivers. The bay has a communication with Newark bay, the Sound, Amboy river, and several others: it receives also Hudson's or North river, one of the largest in

North

North America, it being navigable for floops as far as Albany, above 150 miles: from whence, by the Mohock, and other rivers, running through the country of the Six Nations, there is a communication, (excepting a few short carrying places,) with lake Ontario; and another with the river St. Laurence, through the lakes George, Champlain, and the river Sorel; so that this river seems to merit the greatest attention. These waters afford various kinds of fish, black fish, sea bass, sheeps-heads, rock-fish, lobsters, and several others, all excellent in their kind. The province in its cultivated state affords grain of all sorts, cattle, hogs, and great variety of English fruits, particularly the New-town pippin. It is divided into ten counties, and has some few towns, but none of any size, except Albany and Schenectady, the former of which is a very considerable place. The number of inhabitants amounts to near 100,000; 15 or 20,000 of which are supposed to be capable of bearing arms, and of serving in the militia; but I believe this number is exaggerated, as a considerable part of the 100,000 are Negroes, which are imported more frequently into this province than into Pensylvania. The people carry on an extensive trade, and there are said to be cleared out annually from New York, near   ton of shipping. They export chiefly grain, flour, pork, skins, furrs, pig-iron, lumber, and staves. Their manufactures, indeed, are not extensive, nor by any means to be compared with those of Pensylvania; they make a small quantity of cloth, some linen, hats, shoes, and other articles for wearing apparel. They make glass also, and wampum; refine sugars, which they import from the West Indies; and distil considerable quantities of rum. They also, as well as the Pensylvanians, till both were restrained by act of parliament, had erected several slitting mills, to make nails, &c. But this is now prohibited, and they are exceedingly dissatisfied at it. They have several other branches of manufactures, but, in general, so inconsiderable, that I shall not take notice of them: one thing it may be necessary to mention, I mean the article of ship-building; about which, in different parts of the province, they employ many hands.

The government of this colony is lodged in the hands of a governor appointed by the crown; a council consisting of twelve members, named by the same authority; and a house of twenty-seven representatives, elected by the people: four for the city and county of New-York; two for the city and county of Albany; two for each of the other eight counties; one for the borough of West-Chester; one for the township of Schenectady; and one for each of the three manors of Rensselaerwyck, Livingston, and Courtland. The legislative power is intirely lodged in their hands, each branch having a negative; except that, as in the other colonies, all laws must have the king's approbation, and not interfere with, or be repugnant to, the laws of Great Britain.

The courts of judicature are similar, I believe, in every respect to those in the Jerseys.

The established religion is that of the church of England, there being six churches in this province with stipends (to the value of about 50 l. currency) annexed to each by law. The clergy are twelve in number, who, exclusive of what they acquire by the establishment above-mentioned, or by contributions, receive, as missionaries from the Society for the Propagation of the Gospel, 50 l. sterling each. Besides the religion of the church of England, there is a variety of others: dissenters of all denominations, particularly presbyterians, abound in great numbers, and there are some few Roman Catholics.

Arts

Arts and sciences have made no greater progress here than in the other colonies; but as a subscription library has been lately opened, and every one seems zealous to promote learning, it may be hoped that they will hereafter advance faster than they have done hitherto. The college is established upon the same plan as that in the Jerseys, except that this at New York professes the principles of the church of England. At present the state of it is far from being flourishing, or so good as might be wished. Its fund does not exceed 10,000 l. currency, and there is a great scarcity of professors. A commencement was held, nevertheless, this summer, and seven gentlemen took degrees. There are in it at this time about twenty-five students. The president, Dr. Johnson, is a very worthy and learned man, but rather too far advanced in life to have the direction of so young an institution. The late Dr. Bristow left to this college a fine library, of which they are in daily expectation.

The inhabitants of New York, in their character, very much resemble the Pensylvanians: more than half of them are Dutch, and almost all traders: they are, therefore, habitually frugal, industrious, and parsimonious. Being however of different nations, different languages, and different religions, it is almost impossible to give them any precise or determinate character. The women are handsome and agreeable; though rather more reserved than the Philadelphian ladies. Their amusements are much the same as in Pensylvania; viz. balls, and sleighing expeditions in the winter; and, in the summer, going in parties upon the water, and fishing; or making excursions into the country. There are several houses pleasantly situated upon East river, near New York, where it is common to have turtle-feasts: these happen once or twice in a week. Thirty or forty gentlemen and ladies meet and dine together, drink tea in the afternoon, fiſh and amuſe themſelves till evening, and then return home in Italian chaiſes, (the faſhionable carriage in this and moſt parts of America, Virginia excepted, where they make uſe only of coaches, and theſe commonly drawn by ſix horſes), a gentleman and lady in each chaiſe. In the way there is a bridge, about three miles diſtant from New York, which you always paſs over as you return, called the Kiſſing-Bridge, where it is a part of the etiquette to ſalute the lady who has put herſelf under your protection.

The preſent ſtate of this province is flouriſhing: it has an extenſive trade to many parts of the world, particularly to the Weſt Indies; and has acquired great riches by the commerce which it has carried on, under flags of truce, to Cape-François, and Monte-Chriſto. The troops, by having made it the place of their general rendezvous, have alſo enriched it very much. However, it is burthened with taxes, and the preſent public debt amounts to more than 300,000 l. currency. The taxes are laid upon eſtates real and perſonal; and there are duties upon Negroes, and other importations. The provincial troops are about 2600 men. The difference of exchange between currency and bills, is from 70 to 80 per cent.

Before I left New York, I took a ride upon Long Iſland, the richeſt ſpot, in the opinion of the New-Yorkers, of all America; and where they generally have their villas, or country houſes. It is undeniably beautiful, and ſome parts of it are remarkably fertile, but not equal, I think, to the Jerſeys. The length of it is ſomething more than 100 miles, and the breadth 25. About 15 or 16 miles from the weſt end of it, there opens a large plain between 20 and 30 miles long, and 4 or 5 broad. There is not a tree growing upon it, and it is asserted that there never were any. Strangers are always carried to see this place, as a great curiosity, and the only one of the kind in North America.

Tuesday the 5th of August, being indisposed, and unable to travel any farther by land, I embarked on board a brigantine for Rhode Island. We made sail up the Sound with a fair wind, and after about two hours, passed through Hell-gate. It is impossible to go through this place without recalling to mind the description of Scylla and Charybdis. The breadth of the Sound is here about half a mile; but the channel is very narrow, not exceeding eighty yards: the water runs with great rapidity, and in different currents, only one of which will carry a vessel through with safety; for, on one side, there is a shoal of rocks just standing above the water; and, on the other, a dreadful vortex produced by a rock lying about nine feet under the surface. So that if you get into any but the right current, you are either dashed upon the shoal, or else sucked into the eddy, whirled round with incredible rapidity, and at length swallowed up in the vortex. There are exceeding good pilots to navigate vessels through this place, notwithstanding which, they are frequently lost. The proper time of passing it is at high water. We had pleasant weather during the passage, which is about seventy leagues, with beautiful views of Long Island and Connecticut; and arrived in the harbour at Newport the 7th of August.

This town is situated upon a small island, about twelve miles in length, and five or six in breadth, called Rhode Island, from whence the province takes its name. It is the capital city, and contains about 800, or 1000 houses, chiefly built of wood; and 6 or 7000 inhabitants. There are few buildings in it worth notice. The court-house is indeed handsome, and of brick; and there is a public library, built in the form of a

Grecian

NEWPORT. RHODE ISLAND.

1760.

Grenian temple, by no means inelegant. It is of the Doric order, and has a portico in front with four pillars, supporting a pediment; but the whole is spoilt by two small wings, which are annexed to it. The foundation of a very pretty building is laid for the use of the free-masons, to serve also occasionally for an assembly-room; and there is to be erected a market-house, upon a very elegant design. The places of public worship, except the Jews synagogue, are all of wood; and not one of them is worth looking at. They consist chiefly of a church, two presbyterian meeting-houses, one quakers ditto, three anabaptists ditto, one Moravian ditto, and the synagogue above-mentioned. This building was designed, as indeed were several of the others, by a Mr. Harrison, an ingenious English gentleman who lives here. It will be extremely elegant within when completed: but the outside is totally spoilt by a school, which the Jews insisted on having annexed to it for the education of their children. Upon a small island, before the town, is part of a fine fortification, designed to consist of a pentagon-fort, and an upper and lower battery. Only two of the curtains, and a ravelin, are yet finished; and it is doubted whether the whole ever will be. There are now mounted upon it about 26 cannon; but the works, when complete, will require above 150. At the entrance of the harbour there is likewise an exceeding good light-house. These are the chief public buildings.

About three miles from town is an indifferent wooden house, built by dean Berkley, when he was in these parts: the situation is low, but commands a fine view of the ocean, and of some wild rugged rocks that are on the left hand of it. They relate here several strange stories of the dean's wild and chimerical notions; which, as they are characteristic of that extraordinary man, deserve to be taken notice of: one in particular

ticular I muft beg the reader's indulgence to allow me to repeat to him. The dean had formed the plan of building a town upon the rocks which I have juft now taken notice of, and of cutting a road through a fandy beach which lies a little below it, in order that fhips might come up and be fheltered in bad weather. He was fo full of this project, as one day to fay to one Smibert, a defigner, whom he had brought over with him from Europe, on the latter's afking fome ludicrous queftion concerning the future importance of the place, " Truly, you " have very little forefight, for in fifty years time every foot " of land in this place will be as valuable as the land in Cheap-" fide." The dean's houfe, notwithftanding his prediction is at prefent nothing better than a farm-houfe, and his library is converted into the dairy: when he left America, he gave it to the college at New-haven in Connecticut, who have let it to a farmer on a long leafe: his books he divided between this college and that in Maffachufets. The dean is faid to have written in this place The Minute Philofopher.

The province of Rhode Ifland is fituated between the 41ft and 42d degrees of north latitude; and about 72 or 73 degrees weft longitude; in the moft healthy climate of North America. The winters are fevere, though not equally fo with thofe of the other provinces; but the fummers are delightful, efpecially in the ifland; the violent and exceffive heats which America is in general fubject to, being allayed by the cool and temperate breezes that come from the fea. The foil is upon the whole tolerably good, though rather too ftony; its natural produce is maize or Indian corn, with a variety of fhrubs and trees. It produces in particular the button-tree; the fpruce-pine, of the young twigs of which is made excellent beer; and the pfeudo-acacia, or locuft-tree; but none of thofe fine flowering trees, which are fuch an ornament to the woods in Carolina and Virginia.

ginia. It enjoys many advantages, has several large rivers, and one of the finest harbours in the world. Fish are in the greatest plenty and perfection, particularly the tataag or black-fish, lobsters, and sea-bass. In its cultivated state, it produces very little, except sheep and horned cattle; the whole province being laid out into pasture or grazing-ground. The horses are bony and strong, and the oxen much the largest in America; several of them weighing from 16 to 1800 weight. The butter and cheese are excellent.

The province of Rhode Island is divided into counties and townships; of the former there are four or five, but they are exceedingly small; of the latter between twenty and thirty; the towns themselves are inconsiderable villages: however, they send members to the assembly, in the whole about seventy. The number of inhabitants, with Negroes, and Indians, of which in this province there are several hundreds, amounts to about 35,000. As the province affords but few commodities for exportation; horses, provisions, and an inconsiderable quantity of grain, with spermaceti candles, being the chief articles; they are obliged to Connecticut, and the neighbouring colonies, for most of their traffic; and by their means carry on an extensive trade. Their mode of commerce is this; they trade to Great Britain, Holland, Africa, the West-Indies, and the neighbouring colonies; from each of which places they import the following articles; from Great Britain, dry goods; from Holland, money; from Africa, slaves; from the West-Indies, sugars, coffee, and molasses; and from the neighbouring colonies, lumber and provisions: and with what they purchase in one place they make their returns in another. Thus with the money they get in Holland, they pay their merchants in London; the sugars they procure in the West-Indies, they carry to Holland; the slaves they fetch from Africa they send

RHODE ISLAND.

1760.

to the West-Indies, together with lumber and provisions, which they get from the neighbouring colonies : the rum they distill they export to Africa ; and with the dry goods, which they purchase in London, they traffick in the neighbouring colonies. By this kind of circular commerce they subsist and grow rich. They have besides these some other inconsiderable branches of trade, but nothing worth mentioning. They have very few manufactures ; they distil rum and make spermaceti candles ; but in the article of dry goods, they are far behind the people of New York and Pensylvania.

The government of this province is intirely democratical ; every officer, except the collector of the customs, being appointed, I believe, either immediately by the people, or by the general assembly. The people chuse annually a governor, lieutenant-governor, and ten assistants, which constitute an upper-house. The representatives, or lower-house, are elected every half year. These jointly have the appointment of all other public officers, (except the recorder, treasurer, and attorney-general, which are appointed likewise annually by the people,) both military and civil ; are invested with the powers of legislation, of regulating the militia, and of performing all other acts of government. The governor has no negative, but votes with the assistants, and in case of an equality has a casting voice. The assembly, or two houses united, are obliged to sit immediately after each election ; at Newport in the summer, and in the winter alternately at Providence and South-Kingston in Marraganset : they adjourn themselves, but may be called together, notwithstanding such adjournment, upon any urgent occasion by the governor. No assistant, or representative is allowed any salary or pay for his attendance or service.

There are several courts of judicature. The assembly nominates annually so many justices for each township, as are judged.

ed neceſſary. Theſe have power to join people in matrimony, and to exerciſe other acts of authority uſually granted to this order of magiſtrates. Any two of them may hear cauſes concerning ſmall debts and treſpaſſes; and three may even try criminals for thefts, not exceeding ten pounds currency. Appeals in civil cauſes are allowed to the inferior court of common-pleas; in criminal ones to the ſeſſions of the peace; and in theſe the determinations are final. The ſeſſions are held in each county twice every year by five or more juſtices; they adjudge all matters relative to the preſervation of the peace, and the puniſhment of criminals, except in caſes of death. Appeals are allowed from this court in all cauſes that have originated in it, to the ſuperior one. The inferior courts of common-pleas ſit twice every year in each county, and are held by three or more juſtices. They take cognizance of all civil cauſes whatſoever, triable at common law; and if any one thinks himſelf aggrieved here, he may appeal to the ſuperior one; which is held alſo annually twice in each county, by three judges, and exerciſes all the authority of a court of king's-bench, common-pleas, and exchequer. The dernier reſort is to the king in council, but this only in caſes of 300l. value, new tenor. The people have the power of pardoning criminals, except in caſes of piracy, murder, or high treaſon; and then it is doubted whether they can even reprieve.

There is no eſtabliſhed form of religion here; but church of England men, independents, quakers, anabaptiſts, Moravians, Jews, and all other ſects whatſoever, have liberty to exerciſe their ſeveral profeſſions. The Society for the Propagation of the Goſpel ſends only four miſſionaries.

Arts and ſciences are almoſt unknown, except to ſome few individuals; and there are no public ſeminaries of learning; nor do the Rhode Iſlanders in general ſeem to regret the
want

want of them. The inftitution of a library fociety, which has lately taken place, may poffibly in time produce a change in thefe matters.

The character of the Rhode-Iflanders is by no means engaging, or amiable: a circumftance principally owing to their form of government. Their men in power, from the higheft to the loweft, are dependent upon the people, and frequently act without that ftrict regard to probity and honour, which ever ought invariably to influence and direct mankind. The private people are cunning, deceitful, and felfifh: they live almoft intirely by unfair and illicit trading. Their magiftrates are partial and corrupt: and it is folly to expect juftice in their courts of judicature; for he, who has the greateft influence, is generally found to have the faireft caufe *. Were the governor to interpofe his authority, were he to refufe to grant flags of truce †, or not to wink at abufes; he would

---

* The form of their judical oath, or affirmation (fays Douglafs, in his Summary), does not invoke the judgments of the omnifcient God, who fees in fecret, but only upon peril of the penalty of perjury.—This does not feem (adds the fame author in a note) to be a facred or folemn oath, and may be illuftrated by the ftory of two profligate thieves; one of them had ftolen fomething, and told his friend of it: well, fays his friend, but did any body fee you? No: then, fays his friend, it is yours as much as if you had bought it with your money. Vol. ii. p. 95.

† It was ufual during the late war for feveral governors of North America, on receiving a pecuniary confideration, to grant to the merchants flags of truce; by which they were licenfed to go to the French Weft Indian iflands, in order to exchange prifoners. The real fcope and defign of the voyage was, to carry on a prohibited trade with the French, and to fupply them with ftores, and provifions. Two or three prifoners were fufficient to cover the defign; and in order to have a ftore in readinefs, they feldom carried more. By this abufe both governors and merchants acquired great riches. Very plaufible arguments indeed might be induced againft prohibiting, or even reftraining a commerce of that nature: but as the wifdom of government did think fit,

at the expiration of the year be excluded from his office, the only thing perhaps which he has to subsist upon. Were the judges to act with impartiality, and to decide a cause to the prejudice or disadvantage of any great or popular leader, they would probably never be re-elected; indeed, they are incapable in general of determining the merits of a suit, for they are exceedingly illiterate, and, where they have nothing to make them partial, are managed almost intirely by the lawyers. In short, to give an idea of the wretched state of this colony, it has happened more than once, that a person has had sufficient influence to procure a fresh emission of paper-money, solely to defraud his creditors: for having perhaps borrowed a considerable sum of money, when the difference of exchange has been 1200 per cent. he has afterward, under sanction of the law, repaid only the same nominal sum in new currency, when the difference has amounted perhaps to 2500 per cent.—Such alas! is the situation and character of this colony. It is needless, after this, to observe that it is in a very declining state; for it is impossible that it should prosper under such abuses. Its West Indian trade has diminished; owing indeed, in some measure, to the other colonies having entered more largely into this lucrative branch of commerce: it has lost during the war, by the enemy, above 150 vessels: its own privateers, and it has generally had a great many, have had very ill success: having kept up a regiment of provincial troops, it has also been loaded with taxes, and many of the people have been oppressed by the

and probably with better reason, to forbid it; nothing could excuse the corrupt and mercenary spirit of those governors, who presumed to connive at and encourage it.—The honorable Francis Fauquier, lieutenant-governor of Virginia, who, amongst some few others, never could be prevailed upon to countenance it, refused at one time an offer of near 200l. for the grant of a permit to make a single voyage.

mode

mode of collecting them: for, the assembly having determined the quota of each township, the inhabitants have been assessed by the town-council*, consisting of the assistants residing there, the justices of the town, and a few freeholders elected annually by the freemen; and these have been generally partial in their assessments, as must necessarily happen under a combination of such circumstances.——After having said so much to the disadvantage of this colony, I should be guilty of injustice and ingratitude, were I not to declare that there are many worthy gentlemen in it, who see the misfortunes of their country, and lament them; who are sensible that they arise from the wretched nature of the government, and wish to have it altered; who are courteous and polite; kind and hospitable to strangers; and capable of great acts of generosity and goodness, as I myself experienced during a very severe fit of illness which I lay under at this place.—The paper-money here is as bad as it is possible to be; the difference of exchange being at least 2500 per cent.

The 4th of September I took leave of Newport, and having crossed over the river at Bristol-ferry, where it is about a mile broad, and two other inconsiderable ferries, I arrived in the evening at Providence. This is the chief town of what was formerly called Providence Plantation in Narraganset, and is at present the second considerable town in the province of Rhode

---

* Each township is managed by a town-council, consisting of the assistants who reside in the town, the justices of the town, and six freeholders chosen annually by the freemen of the town; the major part of them is a quorum, with full power to manage the affairs and interest of the town to which they respectively belong, to grant licences to public houses; and are a probate-office for proving wills, and granting administration, with appeal to governor and council, as supreme ordinary. Douglas's Summary, vol. ii. p. 85.

Island. It is situated upon a pretty large river, and is distant from Newport about thirty miles. In the morning I set out for Boston, and arrived there about sun-set, after a journey of five and forty miles. The country, which I travelled over, is chiefly grazing ground, laid out into neat inclosures, surrounded with stone walls, and rows of pseudo-acacia, or locust-trees, which are said with their leaves to manure and fertilise the land. I passed over a beautiful fall of water in Pantucket river, upon a bridge, which is built directly over it. The fall is about twenty feet high, through several chasms in a rock, which runs diametrically cross it, and serves as a dam to hold up the water. There are two or three mills, which have been erected for the purpose of conducting the different spouts or streams of water to their respective wheels. These have taken very much from the beauty of the scene; which would otherwise be transcendently elegant; for the fall, though not large or noble, is by far the most romantic and picturesque of any I met with in my tour.

During the course of my ride from Newport, I observed prodigious flights of wild pigeons: they directed their course to the southward, and the hemisphere was never intirely free from them. They are birds of passage, of beautiful plumage, and are excellent eating. The accounts given of their numbers are almost incredible, yet they are so well attested, and the opportunities of proving the truth of them are so frequent, as not to admit of their being called in question. Towards evening they generally settle upon trees, and sit one upon another in such crouds, as sometimes to break down the largest branches. The inhabitants, at such times, go out with long poles, and knock numbers of them on the head upon the roost: for they are either so fatigued by their flight, or terrified by the obscu-
rity

rity of the night, that they will not move, or take wing, without some great and uncommon noise to alarm them. I met with scarcely any other food at the ordinaries where I put up: and during their flight, the common people subsist almost wholly upon them.

Boston, the metropolis of Massachusets-Bay, in New England, is one of the largest and most flourishing towns in North America. It is situated upon a peninsula, or rather an island joined to the continent by an isthmus, or narrow neck of land, half a mile in length, at the bottom of a spacious and noble harbour, defended from the sea by a number of small islands. The length of it is nearly two miles, and the breadth of it, half a one; and it is supposed to contain 3000 houses, and 18 or 20,000 inhabitants. At the entrance of the harbour stands a very good light-house; and upon an island, about a league from the town, a considerable castle, mounting near 150 cannon: there are several good batteries about it, and one in particular very strong, built by Mr. Shirley. There are also two batteries in the town, for 16 or 20 guns each; but they are not, I believe, of any force. The buildings in Boston are in general good; the streets are open and spacious, and well-paved; and the whole has much the air of some of our best county towns in England.—The country round about it is exceedingly delightful; and from a hill, which stands close to the town, where there is a beacon erected to alarm the neighbourhood in case of any surprize, is one of the finest prospects, the most beautifully variegated, and richly grouped, of any without exception that I have ever seen.

The chief public buildings are, three churches; thirteen or fourteen meeting-houses; the governor's palace; the court-house, or exchange; Faneuils-hall; a linen manufacturing-house; a work-house; a bridewell; a public granary; and a
very

MASSACHUSETS-BAY.

very fine wharf, at least half a mile long, undertaken at the expence of a number of private gentlemen, for the advantage of unloading and loading veffels. Moſt of theſe buildings are handſome: the church, called King's Chapel, is exceedingly elegant; and fitted up in the Corinthian taſte. There is alſo an elegant private concert-room, highly finiſhed in the Ionic manner. I had reaſon to think the ſituation of Boſton unhealthy, at leaſt in this ſeaſon of the year; as there were frequent funerals every night during my ſtay there.

The ſituation of the province of Maſſachuſets-Bay, including the diſtrict of Plymouth*, is between the 41ſt and 43d degrees of north latitude, and about 72 degrees weſt longitude. The climate, ſoil, natural produce, and improved ſtate of it, are much the ſame as of Rhode Iſland, It is divided into counties, and townſhips†; and each townſhip, if it contains forty freeholders ‡, has a right to ſend a member to the aſſembly §: the preſent number of repreſentatives amounts to between 130 and 140; of which Boſton ſends four.

---

* Sagadahoc and the Main, very large territories, lying north of New Hampſhire, belong alſo to the province of Maſſachuſets-Bay; they were annexed to it by the new charter of 1691. The Main forms one county called the county of York, and ſends three members to the council; Sagadahoc, which is annexed to it, ſends one.

† Townſhips are generally ſix miles ſquare, and divided into ſixty-three equal lots, viz. one lot for the firſt ſettled miniſter as inheritance, one lot for the miniſtry as glebe-lands, one lot for the benefit of a ſchool; the other ſixty lots to ſixty perſons or families, who, within five years from the grant, are to erect a dwelling-houſe, and clear ſeven acres of land, fit for mowing or ploughing, &c.

‡ By the charter, every freeholder ſhould poſſeſs 40 s. freehold, or 50 l. perſonal, eſtate; but I believe this article has not been adhered to.

§ Every town, containing forty freeholders has a " right" to ſend a member to the aſſembly, but is not abſolutely " obliged" to do ſo, unleſs it contains eighty freeholders.

The number of fouls in this province is fuppofed to amount to 200,000; and 40,000 of them to be capable of bearing arms. They carry on a confiderable traffick, chiefly in the manner of the Rhode-Iflanders: but have fome material articles for exportation, which the Rhode-Iflanders have not, except in a very trifling degree: thefe are falt fifh, and veffels. Of the the latter they build annually a great number, and fend them, laden with cargoes of the former, to Great Britain, where they fell them. They clear out from Bofton, Salem, Marble-head, and the different ports in this province, yearly, about
ton of fhipping. Exclufive of thefe articles, their manufactures are not large; thofe of fpirits, fifh-oil, and iron, are, I believe, the moft confiderable. They fabricate beaver-hats, which they fell for a moidore a piece; and fome years ago they erected a manufactory, with a defign to encourage the Irifh fettlers to make linens; but at the breaking out of the war the price of labour was inhanced fo much, that it was impoffible to carry it on. Like the reft of the colonies they alfo endeavour to make woollens, but have not yet been able to bring them to any degree of perfection: indeed it is an article in which I think they will not eafily fucceed; for the American wool is not only coarfe, but, in comparifon of the Englifh, exceedingly fhort. Upon the beft inquiry I could make, I was not able to difcover that any one had ever feen a ftaple of American wool longer than feven inches; whereas in the Counties of Lincoln and Leicefter, they are frequently twenty-two inches long. In the fouthern colonies, at leaft in thofe parts where I travelled, there is fcarcely any herbage; and whether it is owing to this, or to the exceffive heats, I am ignorant; the wool is fhort and hairy. The northern colonies have indeed greater plenty of herbage, but are for fome months covered with fnow; and without a degree of

attention

1760. attention and care in houfing the fheep, and guarding them againſt accidents, and wild beaſts, which would not eafily be compenſated, it would be very difficult to increaſe their numbers to any great amount. The Americans ſeem conſcious of this fact, and, notwithſtanding a very ſevere prohibition, contrive to procure from England, every year, a confiderable number of rams, in order to improve and multiply the breed. What the lands beyond the Alleghenny and upon the banks of the Ohio may be, I do not know; they are faid to be very rich: but the climate I believe is not lefs ſevere; and I think, upon collating different accounts, that the ſeverity of heat and cold is not much abated by cultivation. The air becomes dryer and more wholeſome, in proportion as the woods are cut down, and the ground is cleared and cultivated; but the cold is not lefs piercing, nor the ſnow lefs frequent. I think therefore upon the whole, that America, though it may with particular care and attention, produce ſmall quantities of tolerably good wool, will yet never be able to produce it in ſuch plenty and of ſuch a quality as to ſerve for the neceffary confumption of its inhabitants.

The government of this province is lodged in the hands of a governor or lieutenant-governor, appointed by the king; a council of twenty-eight perſons, choſen annually, with the governors approbation, by the general affembly*; and a houſe of repreſentatives † annually elected by the freeholders. The

---

* They are choſen by the new repreſentatives, and the laſt year's counſellors; ſo that each counſellor has a vote in his own re-election. The governor has a negative to every counſellor's election, without being obliged to affign a reaſon.

† Each repreſentative muſt be reſident in the townſhip for which he is elected; he muſt alſo have a plurality of votes refpecting the number of voters, and not in comparifon only of the other candidates; he is paid for his attendance and ſervices, and ſubject to a fine if he neglects them.

governor

governor commissions all the militia, and other military officers; and, with consent of the council, also nominates and appoints all civil officers, except those that are concerned in the revenue. He calls and adjourns the assembly, and has in every respect a very extensive authority. His salary, with perquisites, amounts to about 1300 l. sterling per year. The governor and council together have the probate of wills, and the power of granting administrations and divorces.

There are several courts of judicature. All actions under twenty shillings sterling are cognizable by a justice of peace, from whose determination there lies an appeal to the inferior county-court of common-pleas; and from hence to the superior provincial court in its circuits, which is also a court of oyer and terminer in criminal affairs, and is held by a chief justice and some assistant judges. In this court, if the determination is not satisfactory, a rehearing of the cause may be had with a different jury*; and even, by petition to the general assembly, a second rehearing: the dernier resort is to his majesty in council, but this only in cases of 300 l. sterling value: and the appeal must be made within fourteen days after judgment.

The established religion here, as in all the other provinces of New England, is that of the congregationalists; a religion, different in some trifling articles, though none very material, from the presbyterian. There are, besides these however, great numbers of people of different persuasions, particularly of the religion of the church of England; which seems to gain ground, and to become more fashionable every day. A church has been lately erected at Cambridge, within sight of the college; which has greatly alarmed the congregationalists, who consider it as the most fatal stroke, that could possibly have been levelled at their religion. The building is elegant,

* Juries are, I believe, appointed partly by lot, and partly by rotation.

and the minister of it (the reverend Mr. Apthorpe,) is a very amiable young man, of shining parts, great learning, and pure and engaging manners.*

Arts and Sciences seem to have made a greater progress here, than in any other part of America. Harvard college has been founded above a hundred years; and although it is not upon a perfect plan, yet it has produced a very good effect. The arts are undeniably much forwarder in Massachusets-Bay, than either in Pensylvania or New York. The public buildings are more elegant; and there is a more general turn for music, painting, and the belles lettres.

The character of the inhabitants of this province is much improved, in comparison of what it was: but puritanism and a spirit of persecution is not yet totally extinguished. The gentry of both sexes are hospitable, and good-natured; there is an air of civility in their behaviour, but it is constrained by formality and precifeness. Even the women, though easiness of carriage is peculiarly characteristic of their nature, appear here with more stiffness and reserve than in the other colonies. They are formed with symmetry, are handsome, and have fair and delicate complexions; but are said universally, and even proverbially, to have very indifferent teeth.

The lower class of people are more in the extreme of this character; and, which is constantly mentioned as singularly peculiar to them, are impertinently curious and inquisitive. I was told of a gentleman of Philadelphia, who, in travelling through the provinces of New England, having met with many impertinencies, from this extraordinary turn of character,

* This gentleman, I have heard, afterward met with so much opposition and persecution from the congregationalists, that he was obliged to resign his cure, to quit the colony, and has since lived in England upon a living, (I believe in Surry, (which was given him by the late archbishop Secker.

at length fell upon an expedient almoft as extraordinary, to get rid of them. He had obferved, when he went into an ordinary*, that every individual of the family had a queftion or two to propofe to him, relative to his hiftory; and that, till each was fatisfied, and they had conferred and compared together their information, there was no poffibility of procuring any refrefhment. He, therefore, the moment he went into any of thefe places, inquired for the mafter, the miftrefs, the fons, the daughters, the men-fervants and the maid-fervants; and having affembled them all together, he began in this manner. "Worthy people, I am B. F. of Philadelphia, by trade a ———, "and a bachelor; I have fome relations at Bofton, to whom "I am going to make a vifit: my ftay will be fhort, and I "fhall then return and follow my bufinefs, as a prudent man "ought to do. This is all I know of myfelf, and all I "can poffibly inform you of; I beg therefore that you will "have pity upon me and my horfe, and give us both fome "refrefhment."

Singular fituations and manners will be productive of fingular cuftoms; but frequently fuch as upon flight examination may appear to be the effects of mere groffnefs of character, will, upon deeper refearch, be found to proceed from fimplicity and innocence. A very extraordinary method of courtfhip, which is fometimes practifed amongft the lower people of this province, and is called Tarrying, has given occafion to this reflection. When a man is enamoured of a young woman, and wifhes to marry her, he propofes the affair to her parents, (without whofe confent no marriage in this colony can take place); if they have no objection, they allow him to tarry with her one night, in order to make his court to her. At their ufual time the old couple retire to bed, leaving the young

* Inns are fo called in America.

ones to settle matters as they can; who, after having sate up as long as they think proper, get into bed together also, but without pulling off their under garments, in order to prevent scandal. If the parties agree, it is all very well ; the banns are published, and they are married without delay. If not, they part, and possibly never see each other again; unless, which is an accident that seldom happens, the forsaken fair-one prove pregnant, and then the man is obliged to marry her, under pain of excommunication*.

The province of Massachusets-Bay has been for some years past, I believe, rather on the decline. Its inhabitants have lost several branches of trade, which they are not likely to recover again. They formerly supplied, not only Connecticut, but other parts of the continent, with dry goods, and received specie in return : but since the introduction of paper-currency they have been deprived of great part of this commerce. Their ship-trade is considerably decreased, owing to their not having been so careful in the construction of vessels as formerly : their fisheries too have not been equally successful : they have had

---

* A gentleman sometime ago travelling upon the frontiers of Virginia, where there are very few settlements, was obliged to take up his quarters one evening at a miserable plantation ; where, exclusive of a Negro or two, the family consisted of a man and his wife, and one daughter about sixteen years of age. Being fatigued, he presently desired them to shew him where he was to sleep ; accordingly they pointed to a bed in a corner of the room where they were sitting. The gentleman was a little embarrassed, but being excessively weary, he retired, half undressed himself, and got into bed. After some time the old gentlewoman came to bed to him, after her the old gentleman, and last of all the young lady. This, in a country excluded from all civilized society, could only proceed from simplicity and innocence : and indeed it is a general and true observation, that forms and observances become necessary, and are attended to, in proportion as manners become corrupt, and it is found expedient to guard against vice, and that design and duplicity of character, which, from the nature of things, will ever prevail in large and cultivated societies.

also

also a considerable number of provincial troops in pay during the course of the present war, and have been burthened with heavy taxes. These have been laid upon estates, real and personal. Some merchants in Boston, I have been credibly informed, have paid near 400 l. sterling annually.—Assessments are made by particular officers, who, with the select-men, constables, overseers, and several others, are elected annually by the freemen, for the direction and management of each particular township.

There is less paper-money in this colony, than in any other of America: the current coin is chiefly gold and silver: and Boston is the only place, I believe, where there is a mint to coin money.

I was told of a very impolitic law in force in this province, which forbids any master, or commander of a vessel to bring strangers into the colony, without giving security that they shall not become chargeable to it.

Upon the whole, however, notwithstanding what has been said, Massachusets-bay is a rich, populous, and well-cultivated province.—

I cannot take leave of it without relating a very extraordinary story, communicated to me by persons of undoubted credit, as it further tends to illustrate the character and manners of its inhabitants.

Some years ago, a commander of one of majesty's ships of war being stationed at this place, had orders to cruise from time to time, in order to protect our trade, and distress the enemy. It happened unluckily that he returned from one of his cruises on a Sunday; and as he had left his lady at Boston, the moment she heard of the ship's arrival, she hasted down to the waters side, in order to receive him. The captain, on landing, embraced her with tenderness and affection: this, as there were many spectators by, gave great offence, and was considered as an act of indecency, and a flagrant profanation of the Sabbath.

bath. The next day, therefore, he was summoned before the magistrates, who, with many severe rebukes and pious exhortations, ordered him to be publicly whipped. The captain stifled his indignation and resentment as much as possible, and as the punishment, from the frequency of it, was not attended with any great degree of ignominy or disgrace, he mixed with the best company, was well received by them, and they were apparently good friends. — At length the time of the station expired, and he was recalled: he went, therefore, with seeming concern to take leave of his worthy friends; and that they might spend one more happy day together before their final separation, he invited the principal magistrates and select men to dine with him on board his ship, upon the day of his departure. They accepted the invitation, and nothing could be more joyous and convivial than the entertainment which he gave them. At length the fatal moment arrived that was to separate them: the anchor was apeak, the sails were unfurled and nothing was wanting but the signal to get under way. The captain, after taking an affectionate leave of his worthy friends, accompanied them upon deck, where the boatswain and crew were in readiness to receive them. He there thanked them afresh for the civilities they had shown him, of which, he said, he should retain an eternal remembrance; and to which he wished it had been in his power to have made a more adequate return. One point of civility only remained to be adjusted between them, which, as it was in his power, so he meant most justly to recompense to them. He then reminded them of what had passed, and ordering the crew to pinion them, had them brought one by one to the gang-way; where the boatswain stripped off their shirts, and with a cat of nine tails laid on the back of each forty stripes save one. They were then, amidst the shouts and acclamations of the crew, shoved into

their

their boats: and the captain immediately getting under way, failed for England *.

The 12th of October I embarked on board his majesty's ship the Winchester, of fifty guns, captain Hale commander, for the river Piscataqua, in New Hampshire; and we came to an anchor there the next day, after a pleasant passage.

The capital of this province is Portsmouth, which is situated upon the river: it is an inconsiderable place, and chiefly built of wood. Very little can be said of the province of New Hampshire, materially different from what has been said of Massachusets-bay.—The climate, produce, trade, government, religion, and manners of it are much the same.—There are supposed to be about 40,000 inhabitants, 8000 militia, and 6 or 700 provincial troops.—There are only two missionaries of the church of England, and one of these has lately applied to be removed to Rhode Island.—The chief articles for exportation are fish, cattle, ships, of which they annually build near 200, and masts for the royal navy. These are made of the white pine, and are, I believe, the finest in the world, many of them being forty yards long, and as many inches in diameter. They never cut them down but in times of deep snow, as it would be impossible in any other season to get them down to the river. When the trees are fallen, they yoke seventy or eighty pair of oxen, and drag them along the snow. It is exceedingly difficult to put them first in motion, which they call raising them; and when they have once effected this, they

---

* This story has lately appeared in one of the English News Papers, told with much humour, and with some difference respecting the occasion and mode of the captain's punishment. The author cannot take upon himself to say which account may be most exact, but he has chosen to abide by that which he heard at Boston. They either of them serve to characterise the people, and to answer the author's purpose in relating it.

1760. never ſtop upon any account whatſoever till they arrive at the waters ſide. Frequently ſome of the oxen are taken ill; upon which they immediately cut them out of the gears; and are ſometimes obliged, I was told, to deſtroy five or ſix pair of them.—The foreſts, where theſe maſts grow, are reſerved to the crown, which appoints a ſurveyor of them;—who is commonly the governor of this province. This is not the only expedient employed by government for the preſervation of ſuch trees as may be of uſe for the royal navy; for there is an act of parliament, I believe, which prohibits, under pain of certain fines and penalties, the cutting down, or deſtroying of any white pine-tree of ſpecified dimenſions, not growing within the boundaries of any townſhip, without his majeſty's licence, in any of the provinces of New England, New York, or New Jerſey: a reſtriction abſolutely neceſſary, whether conſidered as ſecuring a proviſion for the navy, or as a check upon that very deſtructive practice, taken from the Indians, of fire-hunting. It uſed to be the cuſtom for large companies to go into the woods in the winter, and to ſet fire to the bruſh and underwood, in a circle of ſeveral miles. This circle gradually contracting itſelf, the deer, and other wild animals, incloſed, naturally retired from the flames, till at length they got herded together in a very ſmall compaſs. Now, blinded and ſuffocated by the ſmoke, and ſcorched by the fire, which every moment came nearer to them, they forced their way, under the greateſt trepidation and diſmay, through the flames; and were no ſooner got into the open day-light again, than they were ſhot by the hunters, who ſtood without, and were in readineſs to fire upon them.—The trees included within the circle, although not abſolutely burnt down, were ſo dried and injured, that they never vegetated any more: and as the fire did not only contract itſelf inwardly, but dilated alſo

outwardly,

outwardly, and sometimes continued burning for several weeks, till rain, or some accidental circumstance put it out; it is incredible what injury and devastation it occasioned in the woods. —I was once a spectator of a similar fire in Virginia, which happened through accident. Nothing could be more awful and tremendous than the sight. It was of great extent, and burned several weeks before the inhabitants could subdue it. They effected it at last by cutting away the under-wood, in wide and long avenues, to leeward of the fire, by which it was deprived of the means of communicating or spreading any farther.—In Virginia (and, I believe, the other colonies), there is an express act of assembly, passed in the 12th year of his late majesty, to forbid this practice.

The province of New Hampshire, I was informed at Portsmouth, has grown rich during the war, by the loss of its own vessels; they having been commonly insured above value.—

The currency here is extremely bad, not better than that in Rhode Island.—

Having travelled over so large a tract of this vast continent, before I bid a final farewell to it, I must beg the reader's indulgence, while I stop for a moment, and as it were from the top of a high eminence, take one general retrospective look at the whole.—An idea, strange as it is visionary, has entered into the minds of the generality of mankind, that empire is travelling westward; and every one is looking forward with eager and impatient expectation to that destined moment, when America is to give law to the rest of the world. But if ever an idea was illusory and fallacious, I will venture to predict, that this will be so.

America is formed for happiness, but not for empire: in a course of 1200 miles I did not see a single object that sollicited charity;

GENERAL REFLECTIONS.

charity; but I saw insuperable causes of weakness, which will prevent its being a potent state.

Our colonies may be distinguished into the southern and northern; separated from each other by the Susquehannah and that imaginary line which divides Maryland from Pensylvania. The southern colonies have so many inherent causes of weakness, that they never can possess any real strength.—The climate operates very powerfully upon them, and renders them indolent, inactive, and unenterprising; this is visible in every line of their character. I myself have been a spectator, and it is not an uncommon sight, of a man in the vigour of life, lying upon a couch, and a female slave standing over him, wafting off the flies, and fanning him, while he took his repose.

The southern colonies (Maryland, which is the smallest and most inconsiderable, alone excepted) will never be thickly seated: for as they are not confined within determinate limits, but extend to the westward indefinitely; men, sooner than apply to laborious occupations, occupations militating with their dispositions, and generally considered too as the inheritance and badge of slavery, will gradually retire westward, and settle upon fresh lands, which are said also to be more fertile; where, by the servitude of a negroe or two, they may enjoy all the satisfaction of an easy and indolent independency; hence the lands upon the coast will of course remain thin of inhabitants.

The mode of cultivation by slavery, is another insurmountable cause of weakness. The number of Negroes in the southern colonies is upon the whole nearly equal, if not superior, to that of the white men, and they propagate and increase even faster.—Their condition is truly pitiable; their labour excessively hard, their diet poor and scanty, their treatment cruel and

and oppreſſive. They cannot but be a ſubject of terror to thoſe who ſo inhumanly tyrannize over them.

The Indians near the frontiers are a ſtill farther formidable cauſe of ſubjection. The ſouthern Indians are numerous, and are governed by a ſounder policy than formerly: experience has taught them wiſdom. They never make war with the coloniſts without carrying terror and devaſtation along with them. They ſometimes break up intire counties together.—Such is the ſtate of the ſouthern colonies.—

The northern colonies are of ſtronger ſtamina, but they have other difficulties and diſadvantages to ſtruggle with, not leſs arduous, or more eaſy to be ſurmounted, than what have been already mentioned. Their limits being defined, they will undoubtedly become exceedingly populous: for though men will readily retire back towards the frontiers of their own colony, yet they will not ſo eaſily be induced to ſettle beyond them, where different laws and polities prevail, and where, in ſhort, they are a different people: but in proportion to want of territory, if we conſider the propoſition in a general and abſtract light, will be want of power.—But the northern colonies have ſtill more poſitive and real diſadvantages to contend with. They are compoſed of people of different nations, different manners, different religions, and different languages. They have a mutual jealouſy of each other, fomented by conſiderations of intereſt, power, and aſcendancy. Religious zeal too, like a ſmothered fire, is ſecretly burning in the hearts of the different ſectaries that inhabit them, and were it not reſtrained by laws and ſuperior authority, would ſoon burſt out into a flame of univerſal perſecution. Even the peaceable Quakers ſtruggle hard for pre-eminence, and evince in a very ſtriking manner, that the paſſions of mankind are much ſtronger than any principles of religion.

The colonies, therefore, separately considered are internally weak; but it may be supposed, that, by an union or coalition, they would become strong and formidable; but an union seems almost impossible. One founded in dominion or power is morally so: for were not England to interfere, the colonies themselves so well understand the policy of preserving a balance, that, I think, they would not be idle spectators, were any of the colonies to endeavour to subjugate its next neighbour. Indeed, it appears to me a very doubtful point, even supposing all the colonies of America were to be united under one head, whether it would be possible to keep in due order and government so wide and extended an empire; the difficulties of communication, of intercourse, of correspondence, and all other obstacles considered.

A voluntary association or coalition, at least a permanent one, is almost as difficult to be supppofed: for fire and water are not more heterogeneous than the different colonies in North America. Nothing can exceed the jealousy and emulation, which they possess in regard to each other. The inhabitants of Pensylvania and New York have an inexhaustible source of animosity, in their jealousy for the trade of the Jerseys. Massachusets-Bay and Rhode Island, are not less interested in that of Connecticut. The West Indies are a common subject of emulation to them all. Even the limits and boundaries of each colony, are a constant source of litigation.—In short, such is the difference of character, of manners, of religion, of interest, of the different colonies, that I think, if I am not wholly ignorant of the human mind, were they left to themselves, there would soon be a civil war, from one end of the continent to the other; while the Indians and Negroes would, with better reason, impatiently watch the opportunity of exterminating them all together.

After

GENERAL REFLECTIONS.

After all, however, suppoſing what I firmly believe never will take place, a permanent union or alliance of all the colonies, yet it could not be effectual, or productive of the event ſuppoſed; for ſuch is the extent of coaſt ſettled by the American colonies, that it can never be defended but by a maritime power: America muſt firſt be miſtreſs of the ſea, before ſhe can be independent, or miſtreſs of herſelf. Suppoſe the colonies ever ſo populous; ſuppoſe them capable of maintaining 100,000 men conſtantly in arms, (a ſuppoſition in the higheſt degree extravagant), yet half a dozen frigates would, with eaſe, ravage and lay waſte the whole country from end to end, without a poſſibility of their being able to prevent it; the country is ſo interſected by rivers, of ſuch magnitude, as to render it impoſſible to build bridges over them, that all communication is in a manner cut off. An army under ſuch circumſtances could never act to any purpoſe or effect, its operations would be totally fruſtrated.

Further, a great part of the opulence and power of America depends upon her fiſheries, and her commerce with the Weſt Indies; ſhe cannot ſubſiſt without them; but theſe would be intirely at the mercy of that power, which might have the ſovereignty of the ſeas. I conclude therefore, that England, ſo long as ſhe maintains her ſuperiority in that reſpect, will alſo poſſeſs a ſuperiority in America; but the moment ſhe loſes the empire of the one, ſhe will be deprived of the ſovereignty of the other: for were that empire to be held by France, Holland, or any other power, America, I will venture to predict, will be annexed to it.—New eſtabliſhments formed in the interior parts of America, will not come under this predicament. I ſhould therefore think it the beſt policy to enlarge the preſent colonies, but not to eſtabliſh freſh ones;

for

for to suppose interior colonies to be of use to the mother-country, by being a check upon those already settled, is to suppose what is contrary to experience, and the nature of things, viz. that men removed beyond the reach of power will be subordinate to it.

October 20, I embarked again on board the Winchester, for England; and arrived in Plymouth found the 21st of November, after a rough and tempestuous voyage.

Farenheit's 1760.   JANUARY.   95
Thermometer.

Fahrenheit		Days	Hours	Ther.	Wind	Weather	Hour 2. After
96	Vital heat.	1	8				
		2					
		3					
85	Very hot.	4					
		5					
		6					
		7					
75	Hot	8					
		9					
		10					
65	Warm air.	11					
		12					
		13					
		14	—	10	N. W.	Quite clear - - -	
55	Temperate.	15	—	10	N. W.	Clouded - - -	
		16	—	20	N. W.	Snow - - -	
		17	—	26	N. W.	Rain and freezing hard -	
45	Cold air.	18	—	34	S. W.	A thaw - - -	
		19	—	36	S. W.	A thaw - - -	
		20	—	49	S. E.	Rain - - -	
		21	—	36	N. E.	Rain - - -	
32	Frost.	22	—	23	N. W.	Quite clear - - -	
		23	—	19	N. E.	Quite clear - - -	
		24	—	25	S. W.	Quite clear - - -	
		25	—	30	S. W.	Quite clear - - -	
20	Hard frost.	26	—	25	S. E.	Quite clear - - -	
		27	—	40	S. W.	Rain - - -	
		28	—	24	S. W.	Quite clear - - -	
12	Frost 1740.	29	—	34	N. W.	Little cloudy - - -	
		30	—	34	S. W.	Cloudy - - -	
	Frost 1709.	31	—	24	N. W.	Quite clear - - -	

FEBRUARY. 1760.

Days	Hour	Ther.	Wind	Weather	Hour 2. After.
1	8	30	S. W.	Sleet and rain	
2	—	26	S. E.	Quite clear	
3	—	21	N. W.	Quite clear	
4	—	31	S. E.	Quite clear	
5	—	46	S.	Clouded	
6	—	49	E.	Little clouded	62
7	—	46	S. W.	Quite clear	62
8	—	49	N. E.	Quite clear	58
9	—	33	E.	Quite clear	
10	—	38	N. E.	Clouded	52
11	—	37	N.	Quite clear	
12	—	28	S. W.	Quite clear	
13	—	52	S. W.	Little clouded	66
14	—	56	S. W.	Hazy	70
15	—	38	N.	Mifty rain	
16	—	35	N.	Little cloudy	
17	—	34	N. W.	Clouded, little snow	
18	—	22	N. W.	Quite clear	30
19	—	25	S. W.	Quite clear	43
20	—	34	S. E.	Hazy	48
21	—	41	S.	Hazy	64
22	—	49	W.	Quite clear	56
23	—	36	N. W.	Quite clear	
24	—	40	S. W.	Little cloudy	
25	—	45	S. E.	Quite clear	56
26	—	53	S.	Hazy	72
27	—	59	N. E.	Clouded	76
28	—	49	N. E.	Clouded	54
29	—	42	N. E.	Rain	37

1760. MARCH.

Days	Hour	Ther.	Wind	Weather	Hour 2. After
1	8	32	E.	Clouded - - -	
2	—	34	N.	Little cloudy - - -	
3	—	40	N. E.	Clouded - - -	54
4	—	51	S. W.	Showery and windy - -	59
5	—	40	W.	Little cloudy and windy -	45
6	—	35	S. W.	Quite clear - - -	52
7	—	45	S. W.	Hazy - - -	54
8	—	48	S. W.	Rain - - - -	50
9	—	35	N.	Misling rain - - -	38
10	—	32	W.	Clouded - - -	45
11	—	32	N. E.	Little cloudy - - -	43
12	—	35	S. E	Clouded - - -	54
13	—	49	S. E.	Rain - - - -	54
14	—	45	N. E.	Misling rain - - -	43
15	—	37	N. E.	Clouded - - -	39
16	—	30	N.	Thick snow - - -	32
17	—	26	N. W.	Snow - - - -	32
18	—	27	N. W.	Quite clear - - -	38
19	—	39	S. W.	Clouded - - -	52
20	—	41	N. W.	Cloudy - - -	38
21	—	29	N. E.	Snow - - - -	34
22	—	36	N. E.	Rain - - - -	39
23	—	39	E.	Little cloudy - - -	50
24	—	45	E.	Little cloudy - - -	52
25	—	49	S. E.	Little cloudy - - -	56
26	—	41	N. W.	Quite clear - - -	48
27	—	43	S. W.	Quite clear - - -	54
28	—	53	S. W.	Quite clear - - -	70
29	—	64	S. W.	Hazy - - - -	74
30	—	57	S. W.	Rain - - - -	67
31	—	66	W.	Showery - - -	64

Q.

A P R I L.   1760.

Days	Hour	Ther.	Wind	Weather	Hour. 2. After.
1	8	49	N. W.	Quite clear	55
2	—	50	S.	Quite clear	67
3	—	61	S. W.	Clouded	70
4	—	65	S. E	Quite clear	76
5	—	70	W.	Quite clear, thunder	79
6	—	57	E.	Clouded	60
7	—	50	N. W.	Thunder, clouded	65
8	—	47	N. E.	Thunder, clouded	50
9	—	45	N. E.	Clouded	50
10	—	64	S. W.	Little cloudy, thunder	85
11	—	44	N. E.	Small rain	52
12	—	53	N. E.	Little cloudy	56
13	—	53	S. E.	Clouded	69
14	—	67	S. W.	Little cloudy	73
15	—	70	S. W.	Cloudy, thunder	80
16	—	48	N. W.	Little cloudy	58
17	—	53	S. E.	Clouded	50
18	—	45	N. E.	Clouded	50
19	—	55	W.	Quite clear	72
20	—	59	S. W.	Quite clear, thunder	77
21	—	64	E.	Quite clear	77
22	—	65	S. E.	Clouded	75
23	—	65	S. W.	Cloudy and showers	76
24	—	69	S. E.	Quite clear	70
25	—	70	S. E.	Quite clear	80
26	—	74	S. W.	Quite clear	84
27	—	77	S. W.	Quite clear, thunder	85
28	—	70	S. W.	Quite clear	80
29	—	65	N. W.	Quite clear	69
30	—	62	N. W.	Quite clear	60

1760.   M A Y.   99

Days	Hour	Ther.	Wind	Weather	Hour 2. After.
1	8	50	N. W.	Quite clear - -	60
2	—	56	N. E.	Little cloudy - -	64
3	—	52	W.	Quite clear - - -	64
4	—	64	S. W.	Quite clear - -	74
5	—	65	S. W.	Foggy, little rain -	74
6	—	58	N. E.	Clouded - - -	63
7	—	60	N. E.	Quite clear - -	69
8	—	60	S. E.	Quite clear - - -	73
9	—	72	S. W.	Quite clear - -	81
10	—	71	S. W.	Quite clear, thunder -	80
11	—	65	N. E.	Little cloudy - -	70
12	—	58	N. E.	Rain, thunder - -	57
13	—	60	S. W.	Cloudy, thunder	70
14	—	68	N. W.	Cloudy - - -	70
15	—	67	W.	Little cloudy - -	72
16	—	73	S. W.	Clouded, little rain -	77
17	—	78	S. W.	Little cloudy - -	83
18	—	74	W.	Cloudy, thunder - -	78
19	—	68	N. W.	Cloudy - - -	75
20	—	66	N. W.	Little cloudy - -	75
21	—	72	N. E.	Quite clear - - -	75
22	—	64	N. E.	Rain,—thunder - -	61
23	—	58	N. E.	Clouded - - -	69
24	—	73	W.	Rain,—thunder - -	63
25	—	71	N. W.	Quite clear - -	78
26	—	76	——	Thunder - - -	82
27	—	61	——	- - - -	68
28	—	64	——	- - - -	70
29	—	64	——	- - - -	70
30	—	69	——	- - - -	75
31	—	71	——	- - - -	75

J U N E. 1760.

Days	Hour	Ther.	Wind	Weather.	Hour 2. After.
1	8	77	—	- - - -	80
2	—	77	—	- - - -	83
3	—	80	—	- - - -	88
4	—	83	—	Thunder - - -	88
5	—	62	—	Rain - - -	70
6	—	65	—	Thunder - - -	63
7	—	65	—	- - - -	73
8	—	67	—	- - - -	78
9	—	70	—	Rain - - -	75
10	—	65	—	- - - -	75
11	—	74	—	- - - -	81
12	—	78	—	- - - -	89
13	—	80	—	- - - -	87
14	—	82	—	- - - -	89
15	—	86	—	- - - -	91
16	—	90	—	Thunder - - -	90
17	—	78	—	Thunder - - -	87
18	—	73	—	High wind - - -	75
19	—	66	—	- - - -	75
20	—	78	—	- - - -	83
21	—	80	—	- - - -	89
22	—	73	—	- - - -	75
23	—	68	—	Rain, thnnder - -	80
24	—	72	—	- - - -	78
25	—	76	—	- - - -	79
26	—	73	—	- - - -	80
27	—	76	—	Thunder - - -	80
28	—	80	—	- - - -	85
29	—	81	—	- - - -	83
30	—	75	—	- - - -	83

1760. JULY.

Days	Hour	Ther.	Wind	Weather.	Hour 2. After.
1	8	80	——	Thunder	86
2	—	75	——	-	82
3	—	81	——	-	89
4	—	87	——	Thunder	92
5	—	75	——	Rain	76
6	—	72	——	-	78
7	—	72	——	-	80
8	—	71	——	Small rain	78
9	—	73	——	Rain	83
10	—	75	——	-	80
11	—	84	——	-	86
12	—	84	——	-	88
13	—	86	——	-	92
14	—	87	——	-	92
15	—	87	——	-	91
16	—	83	——	Thunder	83
17	—	77	——	Rain	81
18	—	75	——	Rain	84
19	—	80	——	Rain	83
20	—	77	——	Rain	78
21	—	75	——	-	87
22	—	80	——	Thunder	88
23	—	84	——	Thunder	93
24	—	88	——	-	93
25	—	89	——	Thunder	94
26	—	86	——	-	80
27	—	78	——	-	80
28	—	74	——	-	77
29	—	80	——	-	81
30	—	80	——	-	82
31	—	72	——	Rain	78

AUGUST. 1760.

Days	Hour	Ther.	Wind	Weather	Hour 2. After.
1	8	77	——	- - - -	84
2	—	77	——	- - - -	81
3	—	75	——	Rain - - -	78
4	—	73	——	- - - -	78
5	—	74	——	Rain - - -	84
6	—	83	——	- - - -	89
7	—	85	——	- - - -	90
8	—	85	——	- - - -	91
9	—	87	——	Thunder - -	92
10	—	87	——	- - - -	91
11	—	89	——	- - -	93
12	—	89	——	Thunder - -	94
13	—	90	——	Thunder - - -	94
14	—	80	——	Rain - - -	86
15	—	84	——	Thunder - - -	88
16	—	79	——	- - - -	87
17	—	84	——	- - - -	86
18	—	80	——	- - - -	88
19	—	83	——	- - - -	88
20	—	78	——	- - - -	83
21	—	72	——	- - - -	79
22	—	78	——	Rain - - -	83
23	—	76	——	- - - -	84
24	—	77	——	- - - -	84
25	—	83	——	- - - -	86
26	—	76	——	- - - -	83
27	—	84	——	- - - -	89
28	—	72	——	Thunder - - -	78
29	—	—	——	- - - -	—
30	—	—	——	- - - -	—
31	—	31	——	- - - -	96

1760.   S E P T E M B E R.

Days	Hour	Ther.	Wind	Weather				Hour. 2. After
1	8	85	——	Thunder	-	-	-	88
2	—	78	——	-	-	-	-	80
3	—	83	——	Thunder	-	-	-	88
4	—	80	——	-	-	-	-	82
5	—	70	——	-	-	-	-	76
6	—	73	——	-	-	-	-	78
7	—	73	——	-	-	-	-	78
8	—	75	——	-	-	-	-	81
9	—	80	——	-	-	-	-	86
10	—	80	——	A shower	-	-	-	87
11	—	80	——	-	-	-	-	86
12	—	80	——	-	-	-	-	83
13	—	76	——	-	-	-	-	78
14	—	69	——	-	-	-	-	80
15	—	82	——	A shower	-	-	-	91
16	—	71	——	-	-	-	-	72
17	—	67	——	Rain	-	-	-	72
18	—	55	——	-	-	-	-	62
19	—	64	——	-	-	-	-	68
20	—	52	——	-	-	-	-	65
21	—	49	——	-	-	-	-	64
22	—	63	——	-	-	-	-	76
23	—	71	——	-	-	-	-	79
24	—	62	——	-	-	-	-	70
25	—	52	——	-	-	-	-	64
26	—	52	——	-	-	-	-	69
27	—	58	——	-	-	-	-	71
28	—	64	——	-	-	-	-	77
29	—	59	——	Rain	-	-	-	67
30	—	58	——	-	-	-	-	67

OCTOBER. 1760.

Days	Hour	Ther.	Wind	Weather	Hour 2. After
1	8	54			63
2	—	54			67
3	—	55			70
4	—	57			73
5	—	58			63
6	—	57		Misling rain	57
7	—	57			59
8	—	58			67
9	—	62			68
10	—	62			70
11	—	62			70
12	—	50			66
13	—	62		Rain	78
14	—	70			68
15	—	49			60
16	—	49			59
17	—	45		Little rain	62
18	—	50			68
19	—	54			70
20	—	50			53
21	—	48			59
22	—	43			57
23	—	42		Rain	60
24	—	63			71
25	—	50			58
26	—	48			69
27	—	50			63
28	—	—		Rain	60
29	—	45			43
30	—	43			49
31	—	30			

www.ingramcontent.com/pod-product-compliance
Lightning Source LLC
Chambersburg PA
CBHW020143170426
43199CB00010B/864